A VIEW

from

VERMONT

Everyday Life in America

HELEN HUSHER

GUILFORD, CONNECTICUT

974.3
H45

Text design by M.A. Dubé
Leaf spot art created by Bonnie Acker
Author photo by Bob Eddy

Library of Congress Cataloging-in-Publication Data

Husher, Helen, 1951–
  A view from Vermont: everyday life in America/
  Helen Husher.— 1st ed.
    p. cm.
  Includes index.
  ISBN 0-7627-2796-9
    1. Vermont—Social life and customs. I. Title.

F55.H875 2004
974.3'043—dc22

                                              2003056999

Manufactured in the United States of America
First Edition/First Printing

for Nicholas

ACKNOWLEDGMENTS

FIRST, AND ALWAYS FIRST, IS MY PARTNER Vince Sondej, editor and critic, who is responsible for all necessary, strategic, and helpful scolding. Then, in no particular order, I would like to thank Pamela Polston, Paula Routly, Joe Citro, Mary Norris, and Christina Ward, and the many people who consented to be interviewed. I would also like to thank the Vermont Arts Council for its financial support, and my boss, Fred Magdoff, who made it possible for deadlines from the publisher to be met. Finally, I want to thank the people who gave me one of life's most treasured intangibles—the simple belief that writing matters—and who helped me to work toward writing well: Helen Whybrow, Vince Sondej (again), Alfred Perry, Alice and Tony Pickman, Alex Gold, J. B. White, and Celia Millward. Much gratitude to you all. I mean that. Totally.

CONTENTS

INTRODUCTION

Nᴏᴛ ʟᴏɴɢ ᴀɢᴏ, ᴡʜᴇɴ I ᴍᴇɴᴛɪᴏɴᴇᴅ ᴛᴏ ᴀɴ acquaintance that I was once again writing essays about Vermont, I got a pitying response. "You are so stuck," he told me. "I totally mean that."

You can perhaps tell from even this tiny scrap of dialogue that I was talking to someone younger and more cosmopolitan than I am, but the plain truth is that Vermont, done honestly, is a hard topic. It's not enough to describe a green, quaint, prettied-up place, a sort of theme park for the rustic life, and it's not enough to go to the other extreme and talk about rural poverty, a commodity Vermont still has in abundance. Like most complicated things, the truth lies somewhere in the middle. The vast majority of Vermonters are neither completely broke nor relentlessly tasteful. Instead, they chug along in the big sloppy middle, being their own unstoppable selves. I like this, and it interests me, because Vermont is a paradox. It is a place, both in space and in the heart, that cherishes and supports the individual, yet also has a powerful sense of community. How this plays out—the details and the character and the history—is what keeps me interested, and keeps me acting on the assumption that it is both my duty and my pleasure to keep an eye on the proceedings.

Some of the material collected here originally appeared in an abbreviated form in the Burlington arts and comment weekly, *Seven Days*, where I was a contributor for a couple of years. In the interests of accuracy, I have to say that I was never all that happy with what I gave them—all the original stories felt perfunctory and incomplete. They were undercooked; cooking takes time; time is not plentiful in the newspaper business. By putting these stories into book form, I have been able to rethink why I wanted to write them in the first place, and I have tried to clarify why the erratic heartbeat that propels the Vermont temperament is worth so much of my time and trouble. If that means I am stuck, then so be it. Contrary to received opinion, writers do not really write about what they know. They write about what obsesses them, and this is not the same thing.

It is this obsession, I think, that drives me to read far too many small-town weekly newspapers, and to eavesdrop, mooch, and loaf, and to call up people I don't know on the telephone. If you're an ordinary citizen, this kind of behavior can get you in no end of trouble, but because I am a writer

it's all done under the banner of research, which is respectable and even good. This same research requires that I drive around on marginal dirt roads and pull over whenever something catches my attention; it also means going pretty much anywhere that prints up a brochure, which I take away and read with a terrible concentration, as if the text were a great work of literature that demanded explication.

Most places don't really stand up well to this level of scrutiny, and sometimes Vermont doesn't, either, as you will see. During this past mud season—a period called spring everywhere else in the country—it dawned on me that the lengthening days and expanding sunlight were not entirely welcome, since it mostly meant that Vermonters had an improved opportunity to gaze out on 9,300 square miles of grubby, shopworn snow. The dreariness of the Vermont spring comes in multiple manifestations: The basement floods, the melting ice backs up under the roof shingles, and—the final indignity—your shoes get sucked off your feet between the house and the car. The only upside to mud season is sugaring, a mythical and mighty time of brave men in plaid struggling in the woods with miles of pale blue tubing; this is the modern way of getting the sap from the sugarbush down to the sugarhouse to be boiled. The places that still hitch up the team and use the old oaken buckets are posing for the tourists, and to be frank there is very little tourism during the mud time because most of the roads aren't paved. There is a minor cottage industry of pulling tourists out of ditches, but that is all.

It's a challenging environment, but it's also an environment that tends to nurture a slightly different kind of Yankee, one who is often bumptious, distracted, merry, and unpredictable. People here matter, not in the aggregate, but one at a time. This can make for an exciting ride, but it's also what makes Vermonters worth writing about at all. Calvin Trillin, in his collection of stories about small-town murders, called *Killings*, made exactly this distinction, and he explained, better than I can, what makes particularity so compelling: "I wasn't interested," he wrote, "in doing what is sometimes called Americana—stories about people like the last fellow in Jasper County, Georgia, who can whittle worth a damn." Instead, he used the inherent drama of rural misadventure to run to the particular, to skirt the platitude, to witness a kind of forced transparency. "When someone dies suddenly," he said, "the shades are drawn up"; when the trial begins, we become "transfixed by a process in which the person being asked a question actually has to answer it."

There's no death in this book, or not much death, but there is, I hope, at least some of the same momentum. I am pleased to live in a state where the shades are often up, and where questions are often answered. But perhaps what really holds my attention about Vermont is that it is not what it is said to be—it's not Americana. Despite many decades of accommodating the carriage trade, tourism here has not yet descended into platitude. Instead, the yearly influx of tired and frazzled out-of-staters always seem to me to be greeted with a kind of welcoming sorrow, as if they were lost kittens. The poorest Vermonter, scrabbling along on two jobs, often feels she is somehow better off than any visitor and can thus afford to be pleasant and charitable; she will even fire up the John Deere and pull their Volvo out of the muck.

But it is, finally, the play between the individual and the community that really interests me, although I'm not sure *play* is the right word. Sometimes it feels like a kind of dance; at other times it's clearly roughhousing. Much of this minuet happens offstage, though later on you'll hear the puzzled bluster of at least one person from away who, when confronted by the unswerving communal behavior of the town of Craftsbury, simply fell to pieces. His observation that he had lived all over the country and had "never been treated like this" was both funny and interesting. Still, what was really edifying, at least for me, was how the implacable and legitimate questions raised by the community protected them from a menace that no one even knew was there.

There are certain emergent properties to Vermont culture that make it genuinely different—often better and sometimes worse—than the dominant national culture, but what sets it apart the most is a kind of tension between the whole and the various parts. It's a good tension, I think, but a little unnerving, and a little like one of those natural history narratives in which two different species feed off one another relentlessly, but always for some mutual benefit. It's not a process I really understand, but I can watch it unfold and capture its grammar, not just because it's fun to watch but also because I worry, perhaps too mother-henningly, that the day approaches when this dynamic will wink quietly out of existence.

The process has already started, not just with the advent of shopping malls but with the loss of farms and the depletion of small towns and villages as well. As the population clumps more and more around Burlington, and as the tract house becomes the default roof over our heads, something essential, intimate, nosy, and nutritious is getting diluted. More and more, people find it easy to replace the long and difficult conversation of Town Meeting with the quick and easy casting of a paper ballot; more and more, people drive a car through town instead of navigating on foot. The face-to-face conversation really does trump the television, but the television is so endlessly seductive. One of the new problems emerging in Vermont is finding people to nominate themselves for town positions like the budget committee, the fence viewer, and the planning board. At least part of the problem is that folks have something easy and amusing to do now in the evenings, espe-

cially with the advent of satellite and cable TV.

Not all new things are bad, and not all traditional things are necessarily good—I, for one, adore invisible dog fencing and am amazed that it really works. But some kinds of newness have a way of homogenizing experience as if in a blender, grinding away the lumps, the bursts of flavor, and the sharp edges of personal conviction. It's not time to get out the violins—if nothing else, I hope this book proves that Vermont culture is still thriving—but it must be noted that at least one person in the state is willing to use *totally* as an intensifier.

Cold Hard Cider

EASTER SNOW IS SOMETHING THAT HAPPENS so routinely in Vermont that it's almost off the radar screen of attention, except that it's funny-looking snow. Sometimes it bounces like tiny balls of Styrofoam or drifts in aimless swirls like dryer fluff; sometimes it arrows down into the black pavement and seems to pass through it, as if continuing on some urgent journey to the center of the earth. Sometimes the sun is coming out while this is happening. Two years ago on Easter, a prism of snowbow arced across the sky, one colorful foot on the golf course and the other foot planted firmly in my lawyer's upstairs window. It was an interesting effect, and it made at least some of us pause in our pursuit of bunny eggs to consider, briefly, whether such a thing might be entirely normal. It's a good thing to stop and wonder this every now and again, because the fractious climate that we take for granted is actually unsettling for everyone—natives, transplants, transients, and visitors. Not long ago a neighbor reported that a group of friends who came up for a wet, temperamental Fourth of July weekend asked her, politely and repeatedly, to light the woodstove. Which she did, and they huddled around it in their thin sweaters and wondered aloud how she could stand it here. In light of recent ice storms, floods, droughts, and blizzards, it's actually a good question.

The social and political climate can be just as erratic. For example, in 1996 a retired Tunbridge dairy farmer named Fred Tuttle starred in a home-grown movie called *A Man with a Plan*, in which a retired Tunbridge dairy farmer named Fred Tuttle ran for Congress and scored an improbable and disorganized win over a slick, dismissive incumbent. Then, in 1998, Fred Tuttle really did run for the U.S. Senate against a fellow named Jack McMullen, a Republican with soft residency credentials and deep pockets. McMullen may not have been an incumbent, but he did come off as slick and dismissive; Fred Tuttle ran an improbable and disorganized campaign in which he mainly proved that McMullen could not pronounce the names of the towns of Calais or Charlotte properly and, more damningly, did not know how many teats there were on a cow. Fred won the Republican primary handily, but then promptly ceded the general election to the incumbent Democrat Pat Leahy, calling him a "nice man."

It was a strange and absorbing spectacle, and it clarified a statewide position about carpetbaggers, but it must be added quickly that it was the slick-and-dismissive factor, rather than being from away, that bothered people most about McMullen. After all, the current lone congressman from Vermont is a socialist who was born in Brooklyn, and the sitting governor when I moved to the state was born in Switzerland. The cultural landscape has to be spacious and fairly inclusive, since so many Vermont residents have had the singular misfortune of having been born somewhere else. Since 1960 Vermont has grown from about 400,000 people to about 600,000, and much of that increase is due to in-migration.

But what, exactly, are they migrating to? When a friend moved here from Utah, he spent the first month marveling at the local news. "There isn't any," he said. He was temporarily correct: We were in one of those sporadic news droughts when it seemed that the lead every night on the television news was some sort of pet story. Someone saw a big house cat at the bottom of the yard and called the news crew because they thought it was a catamount, Vermont's elusive mountain lion—the last member of the species may have been shot in Barnard in 1881, but maybe not, because people have unconfirmed encounters with them all the time. A few nights later, a dog took the spotlight because it luckily ate no poison. Other dogs did eat poison, and there was a brief but quite serious uproar about that, and a lot of free-floating moral anxiety about the sort of human who would commit this kind of interspecies crime. We saw stories about talented cockatoos and animal shelters and cats and dogs that got along. A golden retriever got stuck in a culvert, a parrot escaped, and there was a multipart story about Burlington's pooper-scooper ordinance. When things were slow we even got stories about what didn't happen, so that a headline in my local paper read, NEAR COLLISION, NOBODY HURT.

The inconclusive climax of one of these dry spells in the news department came with a sports piece about blowing up snowmen. It was pure Vermont reportage. A crew-cut and uniformed cadet from Norwich University, a private military college in Northfield, aimed a cannon at Frosty, lit the fuse, and simply blew him to smithereens. It was something to do, and it was great fun to watch, and when the clip was over the sportscaster turned to the camera and said, with elaborate deadpan, "There you go. That's sports." The TV station liked the clip so much that they played it again during the credits.

YET THERE IS REAL NEWS IN VERMONT, and often the news is thrilling. In the spring of 2000, right around our usual snowy Easter, the governor signed into law a bill that made it possible for gay and lesbian couples to form civil unions. The previous winter the Vermont Supreme Court had cleared its throat on this matter and invoked the common benefits clause of the state constitution; the judges directed the legislature either to allow gay and lesbian couples to marry or to cook up some equivalent legal structure that offered the same kinds of rights and responsibilities. The Vermont legislature, with a fearlessness that is still impressive several years later, promptly began a serious public discussion of the matter, knowing perfectly well that things were going to get hot and uncomfortable.

Which they did. There were vigils and buttons and leaflets and rallies and all the other clanking machinery that always comes with intense public discourse. There was also the sudden specter of influence from out of state, and an uncomfortable awareness that others were paying inordinate attention to something other than the state's foliage, barns, ski lifts, and maple syrup. Randall Terry, founder of the anti-abortion organization Operation Rescue and a man with very strong opinions about homosexuality, noisily set up shop in Montpelier, but apart from boosting the local economy by renting space and fax machines, it never became clear to this news watcher what, exactly, he was doing. The bishop weighed in, and the progressives, and somewhere in the middle of all this a pastor in Newport claimed that someone torched his car because of his position on civil unions, though I can't for the life of me remember what his position was. What I do remember is that it turned out he had torched his car himself. It was a weird and inflationary thing to do, and I mention it mostly because it illustrates something about the problems that come with posturing and public display. The car, by the way, was a 1999 Honda. I remember this detail only because I was startled by it—the car was only a year old at the time of the conflagration and was almost certainly rust-free.

But the discussion of civil unions also put our basic, home-grown decency on display. From the get-go, it seemed almost everyone conceded that this was an area where reasonable people could reasonably disagree. Feelings ran high, but people still listened to one another, queuing up peacefully for the microphone at the State House and offering up arguments, personal narratives, observations, and poetry. Agreement per se was not the important thing about it; what seemed important was taking turns and having a chance to speak. Because of this process, some interesting and arresting things were said. One of the most arresting was the observation that, if we allowed civil unions, maybe we should open the box up the rest of the way and consider polygamy. Wouldn't this also fall under the banner of common benefits?

The idea was meant to be shocking, and I confess that it did shock me, but it also made me think. I'm not a fan of plural marriage, but I liked that my resistance to the idea was

probably the same sort of resistance felt by people who were opposed to civil unions. When you share a reaction with others, it's hard to think of them as the enemy. Like the Easter snowbow this is an interesting effect and perhaps not often seen in other parts of the country.

MAPLE TREES, SKI LIFTS, AND RURAL BEAUTY. A lot of time and money has been spent burnishing the image of Vermont as a place where this trinity is in perpetual operation, sort of like nightly fireworks at Disney World or the *Maid of the Mist*, with excursions hourly, at Niagara Falls. And we do have these things—just because the image is reductive and repetitive does not mean the image is untrue. But it is unsatisfactory. It leaves out the cold hard cider that runs in the veins of the state, the astringent, surprising, and mildly intoxicating aftertaste of violent thunderstorms, peculiar place-names, insular gossip, and muddy roads. And it's hard not to notice that cold hard cider is something you make at home with the materials at hand. There's something vaguely naughty about it, something cobbled up, something variable. It really does happen differently each time—if the fermentation valve leaks it can go to vinegar, and if it gets clogged the whole business can simply explode, sort of like that snowman, making an awful mess. If you jiggle it too

7

much it gets cloudy; if you forget about it bad things grow at the bottom.

As a metaphor it has a surprising number of teeth in it. Cider is a substance that emerges from late-season apples picked up from the ground, called drops, which would otherwise be wasted. In my case I used to gather these drops for free from the Vermont Technical College orchard at the top of the hill in Randolph. I then took them to a mill in Chelsea where a man with no hair squashed them under conditions no longer acceptable to the Department of Agriculture but that seemed fine to me. Raw cider, we are now told, is bad for us, even though it isn't, and we are being forced to decide if these new cider house rules should be protested noisily or quietly ignored. But new regulations don't interfere with the wild, winey aroma of the orchard, the satisfactions of gleaning, or the deep pleasure I think many Vermonters extract from making much out of little, which certainly describes the manufacture of this useful, widespread substance.

Much out of little—it could be a kind of state motto, more specific and expressive than our current one, which is "Freedom and Unity." I don't know about you, but I draw a cognitive blank when I read "Freedom and Unity"—it could mean anything, and thus means nothing at all. When I look at Vermont, I do not see these abstract nouns but wonderfully specific ones: a mineral spring, an ice harvest, a

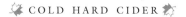

church for dogs, and a mummy's grave. This specificity always hits me with a sharp little *thwack,* like a branch swinging backward or a black rubber wiper returning to its natural home on the curve of an icy windshield. It's definite, and sometimes it stings a little, and it reminds me of cider.

NOT LONG AGO I heard a story about a visitor to the state who ran into the local bookstore. "I don't have much time," she panted. "Where's the next cute village?" Fortunately the next cute village was only a couple of miles away, but the visitor's presenting problem was not where she was going so much as the whirlwind she carried with her. She wanted her abstractions and she wanted them *now*—it's a funny story, and a telling one, but it's also just a little depressing. It's more cheering to imagine this visitor, finally worn out from her many labors, collapsed on a sofa in a local inn or a bed-and-breakfast and watching the news, preferably news about emus running loose on the Shelburne Road, followed by some appealing footage from a commitment ceremony between a pair of lesbians. I want this visitor to worry a little *(emus? lesbians?),* much the way I want my neighbor's relatives to worry a little while they huddle around the woodstove in July. It's not that I want them to feel short-changed, and to not get from Vermont what they came for, because what they came for is always there—maple trees, ski lifts, and rural beauty. But I also want them to get what they *didn't* come for, which is sometimes more puzzling, more piercing, more like a stick in the eye.

This is why, when friends come to town from elsewhere, I become sharp and minimal. I know perfectly well that they would like a covered bridge and a pancake breakfast and perhaps a crafts fair. Instead, I take them to basements and bus stops and tractor festivals, and I tax their patience with tales of No Town, and I send them on forced marches to remote graveyards and strange puppet shows in the Northeast Kingdom. After they leave I become guilty and plaintive, and my friend from Utah, who after a few years has adjusted nicely, finds this funny. "Don't worry about it," he says. "Near collision, nobody hurt."

BUT SOMEWHERE IN THE MESS of Vermont culture, with its burning Hondas, lost parrots, and partisan merrymaking, is a composite portrait of an increasingly endangered place. The danger does not come, necessarily, from urban encroachment—we sometimes forget that much of the United States is still rural, as anyone who takes the trouble to look out an airplane window on a clear day can see. The danger comes, more and more, from the spread of platitudes, of cultural shorthand, and from the breathless demand for the next cute village.

These dangers may be born of advertising and, horribly enough, of Vermont's own self-promotion. By burnishing an image, we have also duded the place up with calico and twig wreaths and plywood Holsteins—you can actually buy these cows and stick them out on your lawn, though I have to confess the urge to do this utterly escapes me. No one will ever be fooled into thinking these are real cows that need silage, vets, managed grazing, and no end of milking and tending. Instead these are shorthand cows, expedient and undemanding, the rough cultural equivalent of the letters spelling out HOLLYWOOD in the hills above LA. They are signage, a kind of caption to remind ourselves where we are. Too much of this stuff is a sure sign that we don't know anymore.

Except we do. This past Easter it snowed only a little, then changed to sleet which downgraded itself to a fine drizzle, which was not too bad, considering. The line for the Sunday papers was long in the grocery store, and many of the people in it were festively dressed, freshly released from church, so that something approximating spring was clearly in the air. Walking home through my village, which really is surprisingly cute, I noticed that someone had put a clutch of eggs under a rather bedraggled forsythia—not chocolate eggs, or even those weatherproof plastic eggs that pull apart and have goodies inside, but round white eggs, eggs of snow, probably scooped from the receding glaciers that still angled up against the north side of every house. They looked quite real in their size and whiteness, and were obviously modeled by someone who perfectly understood the inside of a henhouse. But they were also hopeful and tough-minded and funny, cobbled up from the materials at hand, and it's hard to know whether they were a comment on the climate or just the work of a child who liked the holiday and didn't have anything else to do. It hardly mattered. They were, until they melted, the opposite of a plywood Holstein, and they were, for the moment, news.

Time to a Pig

A COUPLE OF YEARS AGO, a story turned up in the paper about a certain Byron Kelly of Woodstock, who said he had a crab apple tree in his front yard that he thought might produce something on the order of 16,000 apples. That's a lot, but of course crab apples are small. It became clear as the story unfolded that Kelly had lured a reporter out to his place to see what, if anything, he could arrange in his own interest. After getting the reporter to admire the tree and agree there were a fair number of apples on it, he said he was now recruiting people to help him count the apples. It was the year of the national census, and his idea was that these volunteer apple enumerators would gather up the apples, put them in buckets, count them, and then feed them to his cows; this process would give him an independent verification of the true productivity of the tree and gladden the hearts of his heifers at the same time. Kelly insisted that picking the apples really wasn't all that much work. "They're small," he explained. "You can pick up five, ten, fifteen of them at a time in your hand."

The reporter, who appeared to be in tune with the sly, hopeful humor of the thing, played along. Once they're counted, she wondered, what then? Kelly probably had to think about this for a moment before telling her he would pass the total on to the *Guinness Book of World Records.* Pressed for details, Kelly conceded that he didn't actually know if there was a current Guinness record for apple production from a single tree, but that he'd be "looking into it." He finished up this recitation with an account of the tree's history. He and his wife had planted it twenty years before; after that, he said, they sat on the porch and "watched it grow."

I'm willing to bet that most of the people who noticed this story immediately began to wonder how it could be rearranged to suit other circumstances close to home. For example, at the time I owned an inordinate number of large maple trees, and it seemed to me that, since it was late fall, counting their leaves might be a good thing to do; as they were counted, they could be put on one of several ground tarps I own and carefully taken away. I would of course provide the pencils and the clipboards, and could perhaps come up with a kind of checklist for the volunteer enumerators so they could track exactly how many loads, and how many leaves per load, were sent over the bank into a large gully not far from the house. A friend advanced the idea that, come spring, his garden might contain worms that needed counting, and that hardworking helpers could turn the soil and look for them and develop a census report. All my neighbors with big, loose pyramids of cordwood in their driveways were no doubt hatching schemes to count exactly how many sticks of wood were represented and working out why it would be necessary, for research purposes, to stack all this wood neatly in the shed.

One thing that characterizes cold, rural places is how much hard work there is to do and how much of this work is boring. We move dirt, snow, mulch, rocks, and silage, so it's no real surprise that, by the time we get down to the crab apples and the cordwood, we wouldn't mind a little unsponsored assistance. But true as this is, it isn't what makes the apple census story so enchanting and (I think) revealing. Yankees have an undeserved reputation for being taciturn, stingy, and disapproving, as if mired in some Puritan past where dinners are served cold and children huddle in miserable obedience at their work and prayers. This isn't true and isn't fair—the real genius of the northern Yankee lies in a deadpan, potent, and watchful silence. It's a silence in which strange ideas, often worked out in convoluted detail in the milking parlor, get floated like colored party strings out into the world; it's the long, crafty pause inside the Kelly–crab apple story. Everyone, including the reporter, grasped immediately that this silence is a form of posturing, and that this posturing, perversely, is the whole point.

THERE'S A DIFFERENT KIND OF SILENCE at the Brookfield Ice Harvest, sometimes called the Ice Festival, although there really isn't anything all that festive about it. Instead, there's something religious, or at least ritualistic, about the T-shaped hole cut in the ice of the pond, filled with black, cold water. The January coldness of this water, like the January coldness of the air, is utterly serious, and in truth the whole event has the weighty, freighted quality of a Civil War reenactment. The scene here, though, is curiously medieval. A rough wooden derrick with a dangling chain stands nearby, and sharp things and mysterious things sit on tables or in the snow. Clots of children gravitate toward a team of apple-rumped horses straight out of a Brueghel painting, which wait with a terrible equine patience, hitched to thin air. About a hundred people stand in the white winter sunshine, also waiting. If we didn't know this was nothing more than the annual ice harvest, we might be inclined to think this gathering was about witchcraft and dunkings.

This sense of displacement is deliberate and attractive. For twenty-plus years a cadre of interested volunteers has been stage-managing this harvesting demonstration on a modest body of water in Brookfield's Pond Village, and for all those years people have been willing to come and watch the compelling, repetitive ballet of getting ice out of its natural habitat and into a human-made one. It's a reenactment of what *New Yorker* cartoonist and Brookfield resident Ed Koren calls "a pre-electrical ritual," and his use of the word *ritual* is perfectly accurate. If it were not a ritual, it would be very boring. And there are moments when it is boring, and the small crowd begins to chatter and wander off, but once the ice saw is lifted, once the stroking begins and the brittle skim of papery ice is broken by the passage of a huge, neat cube, tremendously heavy and yet floating with a kind of miraculous convenience, everybody comes back and watches with real attention. The derrick with its black tongs descends, the ice lifts, and there is a moment when it hangs in midair that seems full of rapture. People look at it with a kind of wonder and celebration; someone produces a tape measure and announces that the ice is 22 inches thick. This proclamation is met with nods of approval—despite the warming trend of the recent past, there is still ferocity and measurable depth to a Vermont winter.

This annual gathering has been named one of Vermont's top ten winter events by the Vermont Chamber of Commerce, and perhaps somebody, somewhere understands why—it's strange, and it's interesting, but it really isn't much in the

way of conventional fun. It's spellbinding, and it's uncomfortable, and atavistic, a combination of throwback and confirmation—what Koren calls both a historical moment and a social one, in that people use the ice harvest to reconnect with the past and with each other.

THE SEED OF THE RECURRING RITUAL was planted in 1977, when Al Wilder, who then lived at one end of Brookfield's moderately famous Floating Bridge, woke up to a ruckus out on the pond. Wilder got out of bed to investigate and found a handful of local men cutting and moving the ice and calling out directions to each other in the cold—the sound carried well in the crystal air. Before this part of the state was electrified in the late 1890s, the ice was harvested at least twice each winter. Most of the Brookfield ice was sold to the railroad, which used blocks of the cold stuff to keep produce and dairy products fresh during the long ride to distant urban markets. It was also stored in outbuildings, packed in sawdust, for use in homes during the summer months, and Wilder himself remembers the early iceboxes with their thick walls, heavy doors, and fragrant puddles. Wrangling the blocks was an ongoing chore. "They were a pain," he says. "This probably explains why, after the First World War, the first thing most people did was get an electric icebox and an automobile." He doesn't say this sadly, but pragmatically: He's not really a back-to-the-land Luddite who yearns for the olden days. What he yearns for, it seems, is a use for an array of nineteenth-century tools that have stubbornly endured into the twenty-first century. He is mostly a man who doesn't like to see things go to waste, although he is the first to admit that there was something about the traditional harvest that charged his imagination. "I waited for them to do it again the next year, but they never did," he says. "I missed it."

Wilder kept on missing it, and in 1980 he latched on to the idea of harvesting the ice as a demonstration. He recruited a few local old boys—venerable residents like Phil Neil, Bill Osgood, John Harford, and Wendell Savery—who agreed to bring to Wilder's idea the right tools and techniques. "Most of them have shuffled off the mortal coil by now," says Koren, "but they were there to get it started." They understood the ice—not just how to cut it, but its challenge and its implicit test of wiles. "We are still using a derrick that Phil Neil designed to lift the ice," says Wilder, "and the beauty of it is that one person can set it up and use it. It's made so that a 150-pound person can haul out a 250-pound block of ice without needing any help. That's self-reliance for you."

Almost everyone who is involved in preserving rural culture ends up talking about rural values—self-reliance, courage, ingenuity, thrift—and sometimes talking about them with an astringent and judgmental nostalgia. One result of this is that the listener can come away feeling pampered and guilty, as if the hardships of modern life were not hardships at all but minor and transient annoyances. Wilder's ice harvest, though, is different not just in degree but also in kind, since it activates something truly primal and somehow transcends business-as-usual skills like how to make nineteenth-century toys out of rags and corn husks. You can make the toys, often under the rather bossy instruction of someone in a gingham frock, but the main thing you seem to learn is that these toys are depressing and no fun to play with. In my own search for the past, I have rolled hoops, carried water, threshed corn, and tried on some really awful shoes, and none of these things has ever made me want to go back in a time machine. What I usually wanted was Band-Aids—when you visit the past, it seems you invariably get a blister. But harvesting ice is elemental—dignified and demanding. And the result, the huge cube of opaque crystal hanging in midair, looks like the results of sorcery.

For various smart, manipulative reasons, the Brookfield Ice Harvest is advanced under the vague cloak of conducting a contest—if you win, you get a night at the local inn— but for other smart reasons this contest is curiously uncompetitive. When contestants are in trouble, they get help; advice is abundant. Even though there is someone writing down times in a little notebook, there is a complete absence of hurry. There is nothing at stake, and when it's done right nobody gets hurt. It's mostly about handling the tools and respecting the choreography. Best of all, Wilder makes it okay to be inept. When the long ice saw, dark with age, slides through the ice, Wilder says, "It cuts on the downstroke." He says this again for each new ice cutter, over and over. "All the work is done going *down*."

Cutting the ice stops being a metaphor when you are out in the middle of the pond. It's tricky and it's tiring, and the sore-armed contestants learn perhaps a little more than they wanted to know about their rural heritage. A few cut too vigorously, fighting the saw, and will need Band-Aids; experience seems to argue that the advent of Band-Aids was a turning point in human culture. But the pleasures of sawing properly are surprisingly immediate. It's rewarding to feel the saw straighten and come to life as it catches on the white crystal, as solid as marble but more vulnerable and transient, and it's strange to see the block break free and actually float, confounding an expectation about solids that predates nursery school. As the derrick dips and lifts your block, even if it's not an impressive one, it's suddenly very pleasing to be dressed warmly for a day outdoors and to be a figure in what feels like an old and honorable painting. The patient horses dig their cleated winter shoes into the pond and drag the blocks away while the contestants massage their hands. "This is real work," says Wilder. "It's *good* to suffer a little hardship." But he's grinning, and nobody seems to be listening to him.

People do suffer, but mostly from the cold; one memorable year the windchill set the feels-like thermometer at about forty below. The people came anyway, padded and layered to the point of immobility. The only times the festival has been canceled were on account of rain. "To some degree it's something to do at a time of year when there isn't much to do," Wilder concedes. Brookfield is a quiet place under any circumstances, but the quiet in January can be downright deafening.

Silence may be at the center of the cold rural life, and, in theory, silence is what we escape when we venture onto the milky hardpan of the frozen pond. But when we get there, it is often silence that we indulge in; Wilder may be in a talkative mood, but it seems that nobody else is. Exchanges between friends and neighbors are universally muted, and everyone sticks close to the hole, the sledge, the slow-mo action. The hole gets bigger as the ice comes out in cubes, and the cubes are stacked, and the stack becomes steadily more impressive. We are *doing* something, though it's hard, in the current century, to say exactly what that thing is—our day's work is sturdy and elemental but also curiously transitory. If we get a run of warm weather, they'll be gone.

Things are starting to wind down: The fire department begins hawking raffle tickets. When we buy one, we are betting on the date the ice will go out on Sunset Lake, which is a bet about the advent of spring. Some students from the New England Culinary Institute are roughing out an ice sculpture with a chain saw, and produce, with surprising speed, a competent but slightly lopsided basket that evokes Easter. It's all optimistic, forward looking, small-scale, and contingent, but it's also peripheral to the central repetitive drama. Another block—one of the last of the day—is sawn free and then poked along with a kind of majestic slowness down the dark open channel to be lifted, dripping, by the late Phil Neil's contraption. "That's a *good* one," says a spectator behind me, although it's hard not to notice that, in the aggregate, the blocks really are all equally good, and pretty much interchangeable. There is a soft, puttering noise—applause with mittens—that indicates the release of tension that ends a good ritual and is, finally, what ritual sets out to do.

THERE'S A JOKE IN THE NORTH COUNTRY about the out-of-state visitor who stopped on a dirt road next to an orchard, where he saw a farmer holding a pig and reaching up and picking apples, one at a time, to feed to his animal companion. After maybe a half a dozen apples had been consumed, the visitor observed that it might save some time if the farmer just climbed the tree and gave it a good shake, sending the apples to the ground. The farmer gave the visitor a long, neutral look and then replied, "Time? What's time to a pig?"

It's a silly story, but it circulates because it has an off-kilter honesty. Part of the joy of rural life is that time is understood differently, and this difference is sometimes acted out in ice harvests and complicated schemes to tidy up the lawn. But it's not that there's more time north of the Massachusetts border—according to the calendar there really isn't—so much that it gets handled one moment at a time, like fruit for pigs. This can be easily confused with killing time, but in truth it's the opposite—it's meant to keep time alive. Although the results aren't always pretty. A while back, I read about Putney native Bill Kathan Jr., who joyously celebrated the millennium by performing 5,365 nonstop jumping jacks on January 1, 2000. His goal was to beat the previous record of 5,103 held by West Coast jumping-jack champion Steve Sokol, but things quickly got out of hand when Kathan went on to break his own record by doing 5,671 jumping jacks in a row and then broke the twenty-four-hour jumping-jack record with 46,243. After this he set the record for the most jumping jacks in fifteen minutes—1,454—and broke his own consecutive record again with

11,229. Kathan says he is now writing a book called *Wild Bill's True Story from the Beginning,* although how he will get it done is a mystery, since he is also working on running a six-minute mile, all backward.

In the Beginning

THERE'S A CURIOUS STORY ABOUT how Vermont got its name. It supposedly happened during a ceremony on the top of Mount Pisgah in 1761. The Reverend Samuel Peters, Colonel Peters, Judge Peters, and "many others," not necessarily named Peters, climbed up to the summit; the month was October, and Pisgah was apparently chosen because, from the top, the men said they could see the Connecticut River and Lake Champlain at the same time. This symbolism is important, since these two features form what would later become the eastern and western boundaries of the state. This high spot was also described as overlooking "all the trees and hills and vast wilderness north and south." Once the group was gathered, "Priest Peters stood on the pinnacle of the rock, when he received a bottle of spirits from Col. Taplin." He then launched into a secular sermon, "haranguing the company with a short history of the infant settlement, and the prospect of it becoming an impregnable barrier between the British colonies on the south and the late colonies of the French on the north."

It's hard not to notice that this story is in trouble from the start. Mount Pisgah, in Westmore, is one of the state's truly memorable and shapely hills—it sits across Lake Willoughby from Mount Hor, and the two peaks frame the water and pose for some truly spectacular postcards—but the plain truth is that the summit is only 2,751 feet, and it is simply not possible to see from border to border there. Getting a glimpse of the Connecticut River may be possible, but doing the same for Lake Champlain is not, since both the curvature of the earth and the bigger mountains to the west get in the way. Like certain other fragments of the state's early history, there's a particular odor to this account, a tendency to see things that aren't quite there. For example, when Samuel de Champlain first came down the lake that was named for him, in July 1609, he said he saw snow on the peaks around the Champlain basin. He didn't—even the coolest Vermont summer defrosts the mountains by June—but the explorer was no doubt hot and uncomfortable. Champlain also reported that he saw a huge water monster in the estuary of the St. Lawrence River, and, unlike the snows of yesteryear, this vision persisted, since people have been seeing a swimming dinosaur regularly ever since. Mild and useful hallucinations abound here, and this, along with the bottle of spirits, probably explains the view from Pisgah as well as anything else.

To return to the Reverend Peters, preaching on the summit with his friends and relations, the account tells us that he now began really warming to the occasion: "We have here met upon the rock of Etam," he said, "standing on Mount Pisgah, which makes part of *the everlasting hill*, the spine of Asia, Africa, and America, holding together the terrestrial ball, and dividing the Atlantic from the Pacific ocean, to *dedicate* and *consecrate* this extensive wilderness to God manifested in the flesh, and to give it a new name worthy of the Athenians and ancient Spartans, which new name is *Verd Mont*, in token that her mountains and hills shall be green and shall never die." He then poured out the booze and smashed the bottle, giving us our first documented local case of littering.

I'm not the first person to view this account with an amused or critical expression; it was first published in 1807 in the Reverend Peters's *Life of the Reverend Samuel Peters,* complete with Spartans, Athenians, italics, and Etam, the name of the rock where Samson lived while he was feuding with the Philistines. This is, to some degree, the city-on-a-hill impulse that marked much of the early history of all New England. Finding and exploiting biblical parallels was a habit of mind with plenty of precedent, although the references to warring Greek tribes as a justification for a French name are a bit more opaque. It's also hard not to notice that the account actually appeared some forty-six years after the events described, proving that time is a wonderful rearranger. The truth, like the real view from Pisgah, is smaller but just as interesting: Vermont began as an independent republic called New Connecticut in January 1777, but the name was changed to Vermont about six months later, when the delegates to the Constitutional Convention noticed that there was already a New Connecticut in Pennsylvania. The name was probably suggested by Dr. Thomas Young, in honor of the Green Mountain Boys, and somebody got the idea of duding it up a little by translating Green Mountain into ungrammatical French. It sounded cool, and there was nobody within earshot to correct it to *Les Monts Verts*, an accident of history we can be grateful for.

I BRING THIS UP BECAUSE we tend to continue as we began—this story from the hilltop, while dismissed as a bit of puffery by most historians, is one of those transactions that say a lot about preference, character, and style. Because of the way the state evolved, there has been a tendency to worry about names and who gets to give them. It's not unusual to learn that a place was named several times over until something stuck. This is nobody's fault—the whole early settlement of

Vermont was plagued by problems of boundaries and nom-enclature. New Hampshire, New York, and Massachusetts all granted land to various settlers in what would eventually be Vermont, but, because of colonial disagreements, greed, muddle, and the shifting of political winds that blew in far-away Europe, these lands were sometimes in the legal own-ership of more than one person at a time. This meant that some folks had to buy their land twice, from two different royal governors, which created no end of bad feeling. Almost all of the resentment was directed at New York, which had come late to its claims to the region and had been high-handed in issuing patents for huge tracts of land that already had people living on them. Although no shots were actually fired, the ongoing dispute over who owned what was far from trivial. We know, now, that Vermont really exists, but it's easy to forget that it came into being through proclamation and exasperation, with much of the latter directed against Yorkers, Tories, surveyors, and other people from away. The declaration of Vermont as an independent republic in 1777 had a lot to do with jackasses outside the borders, but it also played into a generalized belief that it was possible, like the Reverend Peters, to simply climb to a high place, strike a pose, make an announcement, and seal it with spilled whiskey. Or better still, to just say that the climbing, posing, announcing, and pouring had occurred.

No one was in a position to check, and there was no harm in trying.

LOTS OF PLACES HAVE PROBLEMATIC RELATIONS with the past, but I doubt anyplace has something comparable with the Ann Story cabin. This strange relic is in Salisbury, south of Middlebury, and the building is said to mark the spot, more or less, where an early settler's cabin once stood. The place was picked out using guesswork and historical triangulation, since the original building first burned, then got rebuilt, and then got swept away in a flood. As cabins go it's a sorry affair—the roof looks all right, but the rest of the building wears the empty and patient expression of someone who has died while waiting for a bus. The windows are broken and the mullions are frayed; the inside smells of animals. There is a table under one window with nothing on it. The stone chimney, held together with modern mortar, is silently but steadily pulling away from its moorings.

As a tribute to one of Vermont's early pioneers, it's tepid at best. In winter, when the wind sings a destructive little song in the cracks, it's actually pretty embarrassing. But in the tradition of the view from the summit of Pisgah, this is not really Ann Story's cabin anyway—instead it's an old military blockhouse that was brought to the site from Addison, about

15 miles away, and re-erected in a single day by volunteers and a bevy of kids from nearby Camp Keewaydin. Presumably someone came back later and put up the chimney. This was in 1976, the year of our national bicentennial—a time of fireworks, tall ships, and a kind of misty but curiously militant assertion of our American past. Those were the days, or at least they were different days, and now everyone is a quarter century older, and the house is so fragile that I am asked by the farmer whose land I must cross to reach it not to go inside. "It could have been kept up a little better," he tells me, which proves to be a masterpiece of understatement. "It's better for everyone if you stay outside."

Ann Story, whose house this isn't, was born in 1741 in Connecticut. She was married at fourteen to Amos Story, and in 1774 they moved to Vermont, which was not yet Vermont, but was getting grumpier by the minute. Thus the normal hazards of the Vermont wilderness, which included clearing the land and coping with the horrid winters, were compounded by the uncertainty of political unrest. Then, shortly after the Storys arrived, Amos died, crushed by a tree. This was tragic but generic, almost common—death by tree, drowning, sickness, starvation, and even stray lightning were just some of the costs of homesteading. After the accident, though, the prudent, normal thing for Ann to have done—the thing done by legions of frontier widows before her—was to gather her children, go home, and look to remarry. Why she stayed on in Vermont is one of life's interesting imponderables. Her biographers use words like *brave* and *strong* to describe Ann's response to a daunting world, and these are good words, and we can perhaps add *stubborn, resourceful, immobile*, and *manipulative*. She stuck it out in the house by the river even through the dark and unstable days of the Revolution, when sensible people lit out for Rutland and points south.

What we have so far is a kind of admirable intransigence, perhaps tinged with a high note of desperation. It seems likely, from looking at Ann Story's biography, that she may have stayed in the rough wilderness because she genuinely liked it there, or—equally likely—because there wasn't much for her to go home to. Her father was poor and was "bound out," a sharecropper who worked somebody else's land. Worse, Ann had five brothers and a sister, and turning up back home with five children in tow would have perhaps been viewed as vaguely impertinent. Except for the Abenaki burning her house down and the sporadic visitations from the Tories, it's possible that, to Ann Story, Salisbury looked preferable and perhaps actively good.

But stubbornness isn't heroism, and stubbornness does not explain why Ann Story is still remembered with so many adjectives and such admiration—although I would argue that she isn't remembered nearly often enough, as this dreary cabin shows. Next to the cabin is a marker, placed in 1905, that was erected IN GRATEFUL MEMORY OF HER SERVICE IN THE STRUG-GLE OF THE GREEN MOUNTAIN BOYS FOR THE DEFENDING OF VERMONT. This marker points to a long tradition of Ann Story's role as an informant, supplier, and mistress of a safe house during the unstable years of revolution and national infancy. The New Hampshire Grants, as they were then generally known, were vulnerable, especially after Ethan Allen's rather slaphappy attempt to take Quebec in 1775. The next two years brought the defeat of Benedict Arnold at Valcour Island on Lake Champlain and the engagements at Bennington and Saratoga. The war was in full swing and uncomfortably close.

Strange things come in handy during armed conflicts, and the strange thing Ann Story had was her hand-dug cave on Otter Creek. She retreated with her family to the cave each night to avoid having her house burn down around her while she slept; this had happened in 1776, and she had managed to escape, but after rebuilding the cabin she went on to dig a refuge that was difficult to see, large enough for everyone to lie down in, and included space for food and valuables. And, so the story goes, gunpowder—the Story homestead became a place where the Green Mountain Boys could drop munitions, sleep, eat, pick up information about local movements and events, and then move on.

The cave was partly submerged and was accessible only by canoe; she placed it on the side of the river that was less traveled, on an outside bend away from boat traffic. The entrance was obscured by bushes, and the family's comings and goings left no tracks. As a hideout it was exemplary, even if it was a little damp, and Ann and her children might have gone on indefinitely in these unconventional arrangements if they had not taken in a pregnant woman who went on to have a baby, and if that baby had not cried.

It's never all that clear where oral tradition fugues into fiction, but it's possible that it doesn't matter—there's always some perfectly good, human reason for a story to assume a certain shape. In this case, the reason is a moment of nearly magical betrayal in which the muffled cry of a baby rises from the ground. The recipient of this baffling hallucination was a Tory, Ezekiel Jenny, who was traveling by night to avoid detection. He stopped on the riverbank and listened, and then listened some more, and then resolved to wait until morning to see what happened.

What happened, of course, is what happened every morning in this peculiar household—the Story family emerged from the cave. On this morning, though, they collided with Ezekiel, who made various demands for information and boorishly waved his gun. Story, backed by a nursing woman, a baby, and a pack of children of various ages, cogently but recklessly called the Tory a bully and a coward; there's no question that poor Ezekiel, whatever his political convictions, occupied the moral low ground during the encounter. He shouted unpleasantly for a while, then slunk away.

What's fun about this story is that it doesn't really stop here. Ann, suspecting there was more to Ezekiel's presence on Otter Creek than met the eye, sent a message to Middlebury's Daniel Foot, a Green Mountain Boy, telling him about the encounter. The result of this intelligence was that about a dozen Vermonters followed Ezekiel northward, staying out of sight, and were gratified when he met up with more Tories in Monkton, where they made a camp. Once they had all fallen asleep, they were easy pickings. Fourteen spies were captured that night, thus ending a string of events that began with the wail of an invisible child.

Ann is buried in the Farmingdale Cemetery in Middlebury, and her headstone identifies her as Mrs. Hannah Goodrich, which is really very confusing. It's so confusing that the Daughters of the American Revolution felt compelled to add a footnote: FORMERLY ANN STORY, THE HEROINE OF THOMPSON'S GREEN MOUNTAIN BOYS. So even her identity fell into disrepair and needed a bit of shoring up. For some reason, this Hannah Goodrich business seems the unkindest cut of all. It also seems a bit strange that so persistent a personality would come unstuck from her homestead by the

river, but she did, eventually seeking the comforts of town and remarriage. Still, it's not for us to criticize; she lived in a time when marriage was more urgent for women, and it must be added that she waited until she was fifty-one. When that husband died, she married yet again at seventy-one, securing a brief but probably fairly comfortable retirement.

A DIFFERENT MAID-IN-THE-WILDERNESS TALE comes from Fort Edward, New York, which is an upstate town just east and south of Glens Falls. There, in the summer of 1777, Jane McCrea was said to have been captured by Iroquois, who killed and scalped her. Her Tory fiancé, who was a soldier in the British militia, recognized her hair, which was being displayed as a trophy around the British camp. The story of her death, which to the American press had an appealing whiff of martyrdom, then spread quickly through the colonies. Some historians say that the murder of Jane McCrea so outraged and galvanized the American troops that they rallied with a renewed vigor, and that this feistiness became a factor in the defeat of the British at the second battle of Saratoga in early October. Could be, although it has to be noted that McCrea was allied with the Tories and was actually rooting for the other side. What's much more certain is that McCrea became a kind of poster child for the conflict between settlers and

Indians. Poems, books, plays, and paintings elaborated on the incident well into the nineteenth century, and her death became part of the moral argument, so necessary to the westward expansion, that the only good Indian was a dead one.

What's interesting about this second story is that, like the Ann Story narrative, there's a house she never lived in, a tree she didn't die under, and a marker that fails to mark the spot. These displacements are far more common than you'd think—the world is chock-full of commemorative sites that got moved or were wrongly placed to begin with. In Fort Edwards there's a historic marker and house in the village called the Jane McCrea House, even though at the Rogers Island Visitor Center nearby, the director, Eileen Hannay, will concede that it's a very nice house and a swell marker, "but she was never in the building." The Jane McCrea Tree, said to be a pine, has long since vanished, apparently whittled down to memorabilia; like the True Cross, the number of items said to be carved from the Jane McCrea Tree is far ahead of the available material. Also at Rogers Island is a lively exhibit of artifacts attesting to her celebrity, which really peaked about a generation after she died.

THE DISTANCE BETWEEN ANN STORY and Jane McCrea is to some degree the distance between Vermont and her northeastern neighbors. McCrea, in the progressive depictions of her martyrdom, got prettier and blonder over time, while Ann Story just got older and moved to town. McCrea became an icon, tangled up in the complex themes of resistance and the redemption of the American wilderness, while Story stayed human, hid babies, yelled a lot, and helped catch spies. McCrea is often called "the most famous woman killed during the Revolution," while Story's chief accomplishment was that she stayed useful and alive for the duration. McCrea came to a bad end at the hands of the Iroquois, but she was also getting ready to marry a Tory, and it was the British who employed the Iroquois as scouts and spies. In a way, McCrea died of friendly fire. Story sided with the Revolution, dug caves, manhandled canoes, and quite literally kept Ethan Allen's powder dry.

But it's interesting to see who got the nicer house she never lived in. The McCrea house is three stories tall and offers additions, porches, tidy green shutters, and elegantly preserved windows. A white picket fence decorates the perimeter. It even has the happy distinction of being haunted—there have been reports over the years of the usual footsteps, lights, and inexplicable cold drafts. It is the final opposite of the Story cabin, which is also drafty, but for more obvious reasons: It looks back at the visitor with an expression of almost wanton decay. It's distressing, since, as a rule, Vermonters like to keep things tidy—there's plenty of rural poverty in the state, but most of it manifests as mobile homes with modest, mustard-colored additions and whirligigs on a mowed front lawn. This kind of neglect is relatively rare and stacks up poorly against the swanky edifice across Lake Champlain.

But here's the thing. Even though both buildings share the dubious honor of being bogus, the cabin in Salisbury actually knows itself to be bogus, and this may be the source of its structural misery. It had its beginnings as a blockhouse and was probably used for storing munitions; at some point somebody probably did live in it, simply because it had walls and repelled the rain, but it's not really a sterling example of residential architecture. The only thing really right about it, more or less, is its age. Its otherwise essential falsity may also explain the periodic hand-wringing over the state of the building by the historical society in Salisbury, which seems to erupt and subside every few years without anything actually happening. Richard Adams, the Vergennes antiques dealer who was one of the two men responsible for getting the Addison building to its Salisbury site, estimates it might take a few thousand dollars to make the cabin safe and presentable—a fairly paltry sum, and probably nothing compared to the budget for the upkeep of the New York imposter—but interestingly, he then goes on to say it would really be preferable to move the building yet again, perhaps to the Lake

Champlain Maritime Museum, than to watch it die by inches where it is. "It's terrible," he says, even as he concedes that the modern windows (broken) and modern chimney (unstable) detract from its already questionable authenticity.

Perhaps it is the Story story, in the end, that agrees with the Vermont digestion. It may not have the blood-spattered drama of the death of Jane McCrea, but it does have a good work ethic and is wonderfully free of tinsel. The cabin, unlike the mountain snows or the view from Pisgah, stops short of importance; it misses the mark or, more precisely, fails to make a mark at all. One curious side effect of this is that people tend to talk about the house from a certain distance. This may be because, even though it sits on town land, it's not very accessible. To get to it, you have to commit a genial act of trespass or do what I did and get permission. Plonked on its lot by the river, it belongs, in an odd way, to nobody; the only myth worth reenacting is one that can probably never be reduplicated. I am thinking, of course, of the baby's cry, with its eerie, domestic, and accidental beauty.

THE SOUNDS
OF WINTER

HERE IN THE HINTERLAND, the deepest silence comes after a big snow. I'm sure there's a scientific explanation for this—something about the nature of surfaces and the properties of aggregate crystals—but it's not an explanation I've ever heard, and it's certainly not an explanation on a par with why the leaves change color in the fall. Every September we get the tuneless little song and dance about how the leaves are actually this color all along and we're just now seeing it and how it's got something to do with chlorophyll; it's so forgettable that every autumn we have to be told about it all over again. Silence after snow is probably too transient to warrant this kind of attention, and it seems there are other things about snow that are much more important. Every new inch, we're told, means another million dollars to the ski industry, an economic indicator I've always found dysfunctional, even if it's true. When I look at the transformed landscape of smooth mounds and sleeping trees and fence posts with their white berets, I can't think clearly about money—there's too much interference coming from the pounding stillness and the unexpected curves and the strange snow-odor, as if the world has been bathed in dilute vinegar.

Snow means that it is time to stare out the windows, slowly put on layers, and then go outside and stand in it, holding a shovel. Not much snow removal happens right off the bat, mostly because the world requires a period of speechless adoration of the burial that took place soundlessly, overnight. This stunned worship must be hardwired into the Yankee brain. The snow wars—which are serious business in New England—begin only once this gap of silence has been gotten through, with its roar of nothingness that is both appreciation and assessment. A neighbor's outbuilding collapsed under a thick wet blanket a while back, a sudden event with a messy aftermath, and even this seemed to unfold in a formal and terrible stillness. There was a ticking of nails as they let go, a low groan of warning, and then a dull *ploomph* as the structure dropped in on itself with the finality of an old woman plumping herself into an overstuffed armchair to die. It of course kept on snowing, and the wreckage, with its petticoat of broken roofing, slowly softened its outlines, and there was nothing to do but stand and stare at it and exchange a few amazed banalities. Bad winters—and all winters are bad here—have this compensating goodness, in that we know we are in the

44

grip of something and its squeeze will not be changed by commentary.

Understanding this speechless interval is probably a prerequisite for living here. Every fall, after the first substantial snowfall, the local news crews go out and interview people as they labor in their driveways, and every year it's the same—folks are pleased and inarticulate, glad to be dazzled, sniffling, wet, and wearing their winter boots again. "It's good," they tell the cameras, wearing glazed expressions. "It's nice to see it," they say. "I like it," they say. "Looks like I'll be late to work," they say, but without worry or exasperation—employers know there is simply no point in insisting on punctuality on a morning of pagan worship and pleased immobility. The morning after a big snowfall is an unspoken holiday, broken up only when the plows get through, bringing with them the return of the sound of machinery.

VERMONTERS ARE SHOVEL CONNOISSEURS—we know that it's best to have several different shovels for different conditions. There's the heavy, blunt-edged barn shovel for banging away at the ice, and there's the flat, smooth shovel with its delicate wings, ideal for slicing layers of white frosting into manageable chunks—the snow, especially in February, often has the density of cheesecake. Then there's the finishing shovel, which looks a bit like a scaled-down snowplow, for scraping the final layer of sludge off the lip of the barn or, if you've got one, the paved driveway. Of course not everybody needs all three, but they do need to understand the differences. When David Frary of Royalton shoveled out a horse that got hung up on its belly so that its feet no longer touched the ground, it's a sure bet he chose a shovel that rose to the conditions. With both delicacy and speed of the essence, he probably used a lightweight, high-volume snow mover—flat, grooved, and for some reason almost always a heavenly blue, with one of those newfangled ergonomic handles. I am guessing this only because Frary has shoveled out horses before. Every year or two he is written up in the paper for intrepid, humane, and timely equine extractions. His trickiest save came with a horse that had somehow rolled from the road, over a snowbank, and into soft, deep powder. It landed with its four feet sticking into the air, suffering serious equine indignity. Fast and tactful, the blue shovel with the crooked handle is definitely the right tool for the job.

To engage in the snow wars properly, some people also need a roof rake, which looks like a metal garden rake forged for a giant, with a long, extending handle; people especially need one if they don't have a standing-seam metal roof. These roofs, which are everywhere in this part of New England and now come in a range of jazzy enameled colors, shed snow with velocity and commitment. Huge blocks of the white stuff cascade past the windows, like falling suicides, and land with an impressive *whump* in the perennial border. This onslaught can squash even the hardiest plants, which explains why so many rhododendrons live in little tepees from November on. These structures are often cobbled together from old shutters and the remains of henhouses and have a jaunty, provisional air. Standing-seam roofs can also dump huge loads of snow back onto a freshly dug driveway, as I learned to my sorrow when I put a new metal roof on my complicated, angular Victorian. Even though no individual section of the roof had much in the way of avalanche potential, the sum of its parts, combined with the insistent pull of gravity, concentrated the flow into a massive glacier that cascaded off the kitchen, peeled the paint off the side of the house, blocked the door to the woodshed, and made a puddle in the basement big enough to drown a mouse. And because this raw tonnage of snow lay on the north side of the house, it brooded in the deep shade until June. It made a good fort, and could be tunneled through, and snowballs could be thrown from it with impunity, but when my son and I outgrew snowball fights I was secretly relieved to sell the house and move away.

Snowblowers are largely an artifact of the suburbs, and for good reason—they are a lot of trouble in rough terrain. In and around Burlington, where things tend to be paved and flat, the snowblower emerges from the garage and begins grinding its way toward the sidewalk, and in those two words—*garage* and *sidewalk*—lies a world of information. Farther out, where I have always preferred to live, you do sometimes see (and hear) the snowblower on its appointed rounds. I once had a neighbor who blew snow with a vengeance, making those pristine boxy paths with the clean edges. With 9 inches of powder as raw material, his snowblower left in its wake a miracle of chewing and digestion that we hand-shovelers marveled at, but the fun really began when he got down to the thick layer of mashed leaves, pea gravel, bark, and decomposed kindling that is the default surfacing material in driveways across the state. Then a brown arc of organic matter and small rocks would launch and tumble through the air, hang briefly, and rain down on porches, cars, and vulnerable windshields with an ominous patter. The snowblower would cough once and die, there would be a disagreeable vomit stain on the snow, and this neighbor, an ex-soldier with magnificent posture and a can-do attitude, would sadly take up the old but effective technology. I would watch him hunching over, muttering, and moving the white stuff in what must have seemed to him a table-spoon at a time.

IF SNOW IS QUIET, then ice is horrifically noisy. During an ice storm, the trees crack and shatter like glass—unlike snow, this is not something you can sleep through. It is as if demented sharpshooters stalk the land, pinging randomly in all directions. The low counterpoint to this racket is the dull rumble of brave orange trucks spreading salt and sand. Cars float like ghosts off the road, as if propelled by a magic hand; this spectacle is followed by the high, thin *wheeeeee* of spin-ning wheels and the deployment of flares and flashlights. The power fails; the live lines snake and spark across the road; the ticking of the hard sleet on the roof is like some demented clock that wants to unwind the world.

There is no upside to ice; you can't even play in it. You will fall down, and it will hurt, and there's nothing to throw, push, dig, or roll into an accumulating ball. There aren't even any architectural possibilities. I did once see a kind of rough structure made out of ruined saplings, sort of like a tepee, but it was probably stacked that way in antici-pation of a later bonfire. The sledding is fast but there is no hope of steering, so you find yourself backward, airborne, and headed for the sharp underbrush; if you reach the bottom in one piece, you can't climb back up for a second run. It's miserable.

Instead of digging out your car, you chip at it—sadly, slowly, helplessly—and it's hard not to notice that the technology of ice removal is not very advanced or very subtle. There may be three or four different kinds of shovels, but there is basically only one ice scraper—a plastic blade—and it doesn't work. The flat blade meets the curved windshield and stutters across it ineffectually, leaving behind a whitened, narrow swath of pimpled crystal, essentially unmoved but now opaque; you might as well go after granite with a butter knife. Variations on ice-scraper design include telescoping handles, subtle but pointless differences in the angle of the cutting edge, and—the most amusing—large, hairy mittens with the scraper blades embedded in the fingers. These last are fierce and bearlike and a lot of fun to wear, but they don't work, either.

It also does not work to pour hot water on the windshield. This looks like it works, since the ice melts and steams away in sheets and by the third or fourth application the glass is amazingly clear, but the runoff drips down and freezes the wipers. What's more, it freezes them deep inside the upper dashboard, where you cannot get at the blockage, and it's important not to wiggle the wipers at this point, or to force them to move if they really don't want to, since they break

THE SOUNDS OF WINTER

off in your hand. It also doesn't work to put a sheet of plastic over the windshield before the storm begins. Some people swear by this, but what really happens is that the plastic adheres mightily to the cold glass and shreds itself into strips when you try to remove it, which puts you back where you started with the ice scraper, which doesn't remove sheet plastic any better than it removes anything else.

The only thing that does work is to start up the car and engage the various defrosters, but first you have to get into the car, which is sheeted over, and you must also be sure that, once the door is open, it will close again behind you. The importance of this can't be overstated; for design reasons I am not privy to, the latching mechanisms on car doors are excessively binary in bad conditions. A door, once opened, wants to stay that way, and simply bounces off the frame when you slam it. This means that the interior lights, if they work, will not turn off, and this means the battery will die; it also means that, if you drive the car, the door will swing open on even the mildest corner and give you a yawing and terrifying view of the roadway, close and hard and moving at what seems like an impossible velocity. Of course you can hold the door by the handle to keep it from swinging, but if you have a standard transmission you then have to steer with your knees. This is not good technique even in ideal driving conditions.

But the most interesting thing about ice is that it yanks us backward into a more ancient state. The power, telephone, and cable lines come down, the roads are blocked with tree limbs, the house turns chilly, and the refrigerator turns warm. There is suddenly no microwave, no Internet, no television, no lights, and, if you have an electric water pump, no opportunity to flush the toilet, since the bathtub you filled before the storm hit is strictly for cooking and drinking. For a long while there is nothing to *do*, and there is a restless, helpless feeling of being at loose ends until the chess board and the cards and the Scrabble board are disinterred. A typical ice-storm tableau involves blankets, the woodstove in overdrive, and marathon Monopoly; there is often a patch of yellow snow outside the kitchen door. People live on soup and go to bed early to conserve candles and kerosene—depending on how close you are to town, it could be days or sometimes weeks before the power comes back on again.

When it does return, it is always accompanied by a brief period of weightless amazement, as if the presence of moving electrons is a kind of necromancy. Perversely, this magic must be minimized, controlled, and conserved—the first job after a long period without power is to race around the place turning everything off and marveling at the slack, careless, wasteful people who once lived here. As appliances spring to life, they are squelched with a puritanical firmness—clock radios, now singing and flashing, are summarily unplugged, televisions are slapped off, and ceiling fans are disciplined. Children emerge, blinking, from forts made out of blankets and cardboard boxes; the grown-ups start assessing the damage to the trees, the downspouts, and the shingles. There's a slow resurfacing into the present, with its many distractions and conveniences and dependencies, and the voice of the chain saw is heard in our land.

THE OTHER THING THAT BECOMES AUDIBLE in winter is the gentle but distinct sound of Vermonters coming off their hinges. For some reason, February is always marked by the spectacle of otherwise perfectly normal people doing abnormal things. Out of sheer boredom they leap into frigid water, often for a good cause, but last winter the people of the town of Lincoln did it twice and for no reason at all. A late-winter news item about the annual Winter Carnival revealed that several folks ran from the hot tub, plunged into the New Haven River, and then, "to the amazement of all," plunged into it again. The carnival also offered up a hot-soup kitchen, a talent show, and a parade—"luckily a quick one," the story said—that featured a polar bear, a penguin, some snowflakes, Queen Linda and King Bill, and a pumpkin riding on the cab of a truck. The day finally ended with a couple of people paddling a kayak down a makeshift slalom on the local sledding hill, taking first place in a competition in which they were apparently the only entry.

This is cabin fever. It's not specific to Vermont, but it is pandemic here as winter steadily progresses but somehow fails to end—you hear about people carefully applying wet-transfer decals to the insides of the kitchen cupboards or descending to the basement to visit the meat. A friend, a professor at one of the state colleges, told me she had spent a full week reorganizing her library, sorting the books alphabetically by author, only to learn that she couldn't find anything to read under this new regime. She was thinking of re-sorting them again, this time by color. "I still won't find anything," she said, "but it will look sort of interesting." Keeping things interesting is the whole point. Otherwise, the human spirit turns to drink, computer solitaire, and petty crime: The tail end of winter is when flamingos are kidnapped and road signs are altered or stolen. A few years ago the Vermont State Police were looking for an older-model black-and-silver Ford truck that was spotted pushing a portable toilet down Route 111 in Morgan shortly after Valentine's Day. This apparition was spotted by several people around Vermont's Northeast Kingdom, and a little checking revealed that the potty belonged at a local fishing access area in nearby Derby. It's impossible to know what triggered this bizarre abduction, but we can be sure that the grudge had been simmering on some mental back burner all winter. If you're going to act on your feelings about an outhouse, you are almost certain to do it in the weeks leading up to Town Meeting.

Even the headlines in the weekly newspapers around the state go slightly gaga. Last winter, I began cutting and saving specimens of the genre: TOP SALARIES ABOVE AVERAGE, proclaimed the *Montpelier Bridge* in February; at about the same time, the *Manchester Journal* told us that SPRING IS EITHER SIX WEEKS AWAY OR A MONTH AND A HALF. The *Deerfield Valley News* offered the inexplicable LAMINATING MACHINE NEEDED FOR FESTIVAL, and the *Journal* developed a kind of speech disorder: WHEN DOCTORS DOCTOR DOCTORS, it said. POSTCARD MEETING TO FOCUS ON SPAVIN CURE turned up in the *County Courier*, while the *Bradford Journal Opinion* offered up the weirdly evocative CLARK ROAD TURNS ANOTHER CORNER.

By March, sheer weariness began setting in: ANOTHER PANCAKE BREAKFAST SUNDAY, said the *Herald of Randolph* with a sigh, while the *Bellows Falls Town Crier* told us, ROCKINGHAM LIBRARY AUCTIONS BIRDHOUSES AGAIN. The Bradford paper ran a story called IN PRAISE OF PERCOLATION, which indicated, at least to me, that someone's medication was kicking in, while in the starved-for-novelty category I found DAVID CLARK BEGAN COLLECTING SAP WHEN HE WAS FIVE YEARS OLD and DON NICOLL'S HEAD TO BE SHAVED in the *Valley Reporter* and the *Black River Tribune*, respectively.

And then, in the spirit of this rough season, I came home one day in early April to find a present—a bunch of lightbulbs—on my front porch. Attached to the box of four sixty-watt Soft Whites was a little note: "Jesus," it said, "is the light of the world." It identified itself as a gift from a local church, but the weirdness of it still startled me—maybe Jesus was the light of the world, but these fragile globes were definitely the light of something else, and in this case the light of GE. One thing was clear: Whoever cooked up this idea was definitely in some sort of trouble. But I was glad for the bulbs and used them to scare away the dark, and it seems that not too long after that we had our first freak warm day, with snowmelt running off the eaves and the bats stirring in the walls of the storage area above the woodshed. My teenage son reported that the river was rising, flowing over the ice and up onto the baseball field, and also that someone had been mudholing up on the Ridge Road—this is an activity that requires a sunny stretch, a pickup, and nothing else to do. Spring had arrived.

THE EDGE OF
THE CLEARING

VERMONTERS ARE ABNORMALLY HARDY. In colonial times they held off the French, the Tories, the Indians, and the steady press of the wilderness, and before the turn of the last century they managed to cut down pretty much every tree in the entire state. This was a big load of hard work, but the early Vermonters went at it with gusto—they needed cleared agricultural land. Still, this strategy of cutting down everything in sight eventually blew up in their hands. Vermont is not flat, and the topsoil tended to wash away if there was nothing holding it in place. Despite this drawback, the Vermonters just kept on cutting. They had their reasons, but it's hard to understate the devastation wrought by this overcommitted ax wielding: Old photographs show hillsides covered with slash and stubble, and one source estimates that, by the turn of the century, 70 percent of the land was denuded and there was a 92 percent drop in wheat production because the soil was played out. This clearing also revealed an amazing abundance of rocks, which is another impediment to agriculture. They were used for walls—it's been estimated that there may be 100,000 miles of stone wall in rural New England—but not all of them were used, since there are still plenty of rocks left over.

The main thing that drove this intense deforestation was money. Farming has always been important here, although in the hill country, which is most of the state, it tended to be farming of the hardscrabble variety. But logging paid well: During the nineteenth century dressed timber went south to meet a rising demand for construction lumber, and cordwood stayed here to feed not just the kitchen stove but also to power the expanding network of railroads. Steam engines were ravenous, burning about a cord of wood every 20 miles, and these same engines also drove an economic transformation. Much like today's interstate highways, the railroads brought with them corridors of relative wealth, since farm products such as wool, milk, and cheese could get to urban markets quickly. This was a boon to farmers, but the downside was that the railroads made it much easier for people to move away. This depopulation wasn't trivial. Whole towns disappeared, and by 1860 more than 40 percent of the native-born Vermonters had vamoosed, lured away by the opportunities downcountry and farther west, where there was a possibility of escaping the harsh winters, the marginal farmland, and the everlasting rocks.

But a third thing was also operating, and a more subtle thing: The thick, forested landscape, even as it was dwindling, was understood to be full of critters and noises and mysteries. Its sheer density made it hard to see what was coming, and anxiety and an eagerness to control the landscape made it easy to keep on chopping, even after it was obvious that it was bad for the soil and worsened droughts and flooding. This anxiety was part of the frontier mentality—Vermont was the frontier then, and in some strange ways it still is—but Vermont also has a creepy dimension. Things happen in the forest here, and there's a long tradition, both written and oral, of unsettling events and encounters among the trees. Edward Miller and Frederic Wells, in their *History of Ryegate, Vermont*, tell the story of Elizabeth McCallum, the teenage daughter of two of the area's original settlers. One July morning she set off on horseback for a neighboring farm a few miles away that was owned by the McNab family. It took her a long time to get there; once she arrived, she told the McNabs that she had heard strange music in the woods, strains of a wild melody that seemed to come from all directions. The music, she said, was hauntingly beautiful; she had sat on her horse and listened for a long time, until eventually it faded away. She described the spot where the music had surrounded her in some detail, and John McNab recognized it. Elizabeth's affect after her encounter in the woods was described as "agitated and full of wonder."

When it came time for Elizabeth to head home, she got on her horse and re-entered the woods. I think we all know what happened next—there's a formulaic and well-worn structure to stories like this one, though it seems to be a structure we never get tired of. After dark had fallen, and after many hours of waiting for Elizabeth to return to the home farm, a search was mounted. Within an hour her horse was found, and soon after that Elizabeth herself was also found. She was dead, of course, and for no apparent reason, since there was no sign of blood, broken bones, or bruising. She was lying in the underbrush at the same spot she'd described to John McNab, the spot where she'd heard that sourceless and lovely music.

I like this story because it isn't ugly—so many of the stories about the Vermont woods are disturbed and disfigured. There are accounts of strange reptiles, specters, monstrous birds, huge orange worms, giants, and Little People. There's even a rather worrisome biped covered in pale hair and with the face of a pig—this last was sighted in Northfield as late as the 1970s, rummaging around in somebody's garbage cans, proving that even horrible things must eat. There are stories of banshees, ghouls, and cursed buried treasure, all part of a long Vermont tradition of bad things in the woods.

A writer and friend, Joe Citro, collects these tales and seems to agree with me that the need to conjure monsters is unusually pronounced in New England and especially Vermont. We also agree that these stories say something specific about the Yankee temperament, but we differ a little on the source: Citro thinks at least some of these beings and events defy natural explanations and perhaps need supernatural ones, while I think explanations can be found in the way we think about the wilderness and react to the rustle of things in it that are half hidden and hard to identify. This is why I am attracted to the stories that include strains of music and even enchanted villages that flicker in and out of existence, leaving only voices hanging in the air. Not everything in the woods is necessarily hostile, although much of it is unsettling.

ONE OF THE MOST TALKED-ABOUT WILD THINGS in the Vermont woods is sinuous, elusive, and pale gold. The Vermont catamount—our regional name for a mountain lion—is said to be extinct, the last known specimen having been shot on Thanksgiving Day in Barnard in 1881. It was a famous execution, and it generated a famous picture; I'm not sure you can reach the age of majority in Vermont without having seen, commented on, and perhaps written a brief essay about the languid image of Alexander Crowell,

61

propped up by a stump, with the equally languid catamount stretched out in front of him on the ground. They both look tired, as if the publicity surrounding the shooting was just a bit much, and perhaps it was. The "monster panther," as it came to be known, toured all over the state before its stuffed corpse ended up in the lobby of the Pavilion Building in Montpelier. Many generations of Vermonters have visited this creature in its glass case, and while it's not a handsome piece of taxidermy—it's tatty and cross-eyed—it does have a kind of mythic charm. It's large—alive, this particular cat weighed 181 pounds—and it has somehow retained a slinky and disturbing presence, at once intimate and wild.

Seeing a catamount is a curious honor, and it happens anywhere from thirty to sixty times a year. Sightings come in bunches. Greg Rainville, a St. Albans–based lawyer, saw a large, muscular cat in the hay field of his Franklin farm in 1997, and after the story made the paper he was deluged with calls from people who had also seen big cats. "It's something that sticks in people's minds," Rainville told the *Burlington Free Press.* "It's something that people wonder about." He's right. Over the years there have been cats in the sugarbush, cats in the wood slash at the edges of clearings, cats by the reservoir, cats crossing the roadways, and cats in silhouette against the evening sky. All these sightings are tinged with wonder; the catamount is a shimmering, ideal presence in the public imagination. It is so elegant, so rejecting of humans, so other, and so gloriously wild that it makes a redemptive claim on the landscape. It is a blessing and not, as many woodland beings are, a curse, and it would never stoop to ordinary monsterhood and poke through the trash.

The catamount, like the sweet, dangerous music, tells us something important about the potentiality of the Vermont landscape. Vermont, like most of northern New England, has regrown and covered up the environmental damage wrought by clear-cutting and is now a perfect reversal of the state it was in a hundred years ago. Then, 70 percent of the land was cleared; now, 70 percent of it is forest again. This marks a return not just to a prior Edenic state but to the gradual arrival of a new one, in which the tough and pragmatic Vermonter can entertain an uneasy and complicated romanticism: That which once scared us silly could be renamed as sublime.

NOT FAR FROM WHERE I–189, a big feeder road into Burlington, collides with a minor explosion into the equally frantic Shelburne Road, something has emerged from the woods wearing an ancient, enigmatic smile. In an intersection largely noted for its traffic lights, sign clutter, fumes, and impatient drivers, an idea has materialized, combing the leaves from its long hair and setting up housekeeping. I AM PRETENDING I AM A BUS STOP, it says to the noisy road. YOU DECIDE FOR YOURSELF WHAT I REALLY AM.

This manifestation, which is masquerading as a tiny park, gives about half the people I have talked to about it the total creeps. While I was there, an older gentleman from the immediate neighborhood simply refused to sit in it, and stood almost angrily at the curb. "If you like it," he said when I asked him about it, "you're welcome to it." He's got a point: The effect of being in the park is much like standing inside a Stonehenge of monsters. Two concentric circles of creatures turn their blank, calm faces toward each other so that they seem to catch the visitor in a kind of artistic cross-fire. They offer human faces, folded wings, and big cat bodies. They sit on tall pillars and gaze down, while on the benches another array of hybrids gazes up. Some have two faces with two slightly different expressions; others have long ropes of braided, curiously breadlike hair. All have an excess of toes ranked neatly in feline rows. Vines grow up the columns and twine over these toes, and a central circular grove of trees is clearly meant to be sacred—it's a miniature and symbolic forest that lies at the center of a compact world, and around it and in it these sphinxes pass the time by perching, watching, and waiting. Whatever these creatures are, they are not familiar, and they look back at the viewer with untamed, alien sweetness, their faces full of inquiry. It's unsettling—the sphinx, after all, is a creature that asks questions, often hard questions, but never answers them.

The guilty party here is the Burlington sculptor Leslie Fry, who teamed up with the landscape architect Steven Schenker to create this distinct and disturbing space. They had each submitted separate designs in response to a call from Burlington City Arts, and, in an unusual move, the jury asked if they would consider combining their ideas in a kind of artistic shotgun wedding. Yet both artists say that the park became, in time, a true collaboration. "We both wanted many of the same things," says Schenker. "We wanted something completely integrated. We didn't think the world really needed another park with another bit of sculpture in it. What it needed was a moment of cohesion, a place that looked like it had always been there."

Leslie Fry agrees. The monsters, to her way of thinking, are not monstrous at all, but ambassadors from another, older world. She conceived of them as feline, female, and essentially protective—they may be unsettling hybrids, but they sit with their wings neatly folded. That the effect is a little disturbing does not worry her. "Most public art gets compromised," she says. "It's often very site-specific, and is put there to mark something that happened in the past, or it's there to decorate. Those things just don't interest me."

What seems to interest Fry instead is the merging of something ancient into the present, and to give us a long look at something older and more powerful than ourselves.

In a way it's an act of postmodern archaeology—we're short on artifacts here in the New World, and cohesion and a sense of permanence are particularly lacking on this stretch of road, which is rapidly devolving into generica, that new word for a new place that looks like every other place. Generica springs up on the edges of cities and feeds our demand for new stuff and low prices, but it also strips places of their distinction, so that this particular stretch of Vermont has become indistinguishable from parts of New Jersey. Strip malls, chain stores, drive-thrus, french fries, and the windy plains of black parking lots run for several miles—it's dismal but apparently unstoppable and acts as a new kind of deforestation, since it erodes away all the reasons we have for living here. Obviously, most Vermonters do not like it. But a lot of Vermonters don't like this weird little park, either. It feels primal and upsetting, offering up the siren, the gargoyle, and the outlines of that thing that sometimes appears at the edge of the clearing just long enough to be seen.

We know who to blame for generica, and it's always that evil demon, the developer, who wants to pave over paradise. Yet the third guilty party on this park, after the sculptor and the landscaper, is a developer, the very entity that sponsors generica in the first place. Ernie Pomerleau, president of Pomerleau Real Estate, not only bankrolled the park but also went out on something of a limb with it—he had seen other small urban parks, and liked them, and saw in them an opportunity to do something new. "I wanted one," he says—Pomerleau is a blunt, cut-to-the-chase kind of guy—"and I wanted a local artist to do it." To get what he wanted, he turned to Burlington City Arts, which had, happily, the energy and the infrastructure to pull together the neighbors, the artists, the various city offices, and the selection jury. At first, Pomerleau was just the guy with the land and the money. He didn't stay in that comfortable box, though; Pomerleau soon became not just an angel but a driving force to get it done as well. "Ernie really wanted something different," says Doreen Kraft of City Arts. "He wanted something that recognized that there is something cohesive going on there, that there's a place and a neighborhood, even though you don't always sense its presence from the road. He's a visionary developer."

If you asked Ernie Pomerleau outright if he is a visionary, he'd probably find the idea entertaining. "I won't pretend that this park didn't serve my interests," he says. "It did." It must be added that Pomerleau's interests are scattered all over the Vermont landscape. Several generations of native-born Pomerleaus have been buying, selling, and generally fooling around with real estate all around Burlington and beyond; this family is a pack of go-getters with lots of dough. But it should be added, speedily, that this family is also known and widely admired for its periodic outbursts of generosity, often tinged with exactly this kind of philanthropic glee. "We own the shopping center," Pomerleau says, "which we were rebuilding, and the site is in a neighborhood planning zone. So I had an obligation to consult with the neighbors and the city, and I liked the idea of having a partnership in place. And, frankly, that partnership really helped the planning and permitting process. But what was great was the synergy—we had artists, neighbors, planners, city leaders, and contractors all converging on this project, everyone talking and working together. I have to say it was an awful lot of fun."

Caught up with the rich weirdness of the design concept, Pomerleau boosted the $15,000 budget up to about $70,000 to make sure the execution wouldn't suffer. He drew on family foundation funds and, when the park was complete, dedicated it to the memory of his two sisters, Ellen and Anne Marie, who had died in 1983 and 1997, respectively.

"I know that not everybody likes it," says Pomerleau. "Someone once told me they thought it was satanic, but I don't agree. I think it's just different—interactive and warm. The original idea of just having some bushes and some benches and a bit of art really lost its appeal when I saw what the artists were doing with this design. But it is challenging, and some people I have talked to are surprised to learn that I had veto power over the design and never wanted to use it. But why would I?"

Art is a mirror, which probably explains why the best art makes us uncomfortable and almost always closes to mixed reviews. Leslie Fry, the creator of the winged cat women, speaks about the imagery she made for the park with complicated affection, as if the statues are her beautiful and wayward children. And perhaps they are. "After I finished the first clay models, someone remarked how much their faces looked like me." She pauses. "Maybe they do." And even though she didn't set out to scare anyone, she clearly doesn't mind that the park gets under some skins here and there. The winged cats with their female faces are the keepers of a distinctly female, feline mystery. "We wanted to create a sanctuary and evoke an older, classical world," she says, "and to weave the sculptures and the architecture together so that being in the park would be a seamless experience." Shortly after the park was completed, Fry accepted a faculty position in faraway Florida, which was both an opportunity and a burden for this Vermont native. "I think of it as my going-away present," she says. "I'll come home every summer, but the timing of the

project gave it extra meaning. I wanted to say farewell, and that's how creating this park felt to me."

THE PARK IS NOT OFFERING AN ARRAY of literal catamounts or woodland beings, but it does drag us backward, into a more interesting, mysterious, and animate world. It's a world that many Vermonters want to see operating outside their windows, and shortly after Fry decamped for Florida, the cat-sighting season got into full swing again. In July a group of people on mountain bikes saw a big cat near Wrightsville Beach, and a few weeks later there was another visitation in the same area, behind the outhouses. The *Montpelier Bridge* ran a feature story that raised the question, again, about whether the catamount was really extinct or just lying low and recounted the evidence offered by tracker and hunting guide Jim Paige, who said he had seen the catamount twice while practicing his profession. During one of those sightings, he even had time to deploy his binoculars, and he reports that the animal had a tawny head, rounded ears, a 3-foot tail, and, in a bizarre and almost self-defeating departure from the usual script, that it also wore a collar. Paige said it was a "radio-telemetry collar," and this elaboration puts Paige firmly in the camp of our home-grown conspiracy theorists—there is a curious and widespread feeling that state wildlife officials know that cats are here and are conducting hush-hush tracking operations. This is paranoid but perhaps not all that surprising; plenty of Vermonters are suspicious by nature and perk up at the thought of second gunmen and grassy knolls. Still, it really was a good summer for magical felines. There was a string of excited reports from the Swanton area after a large track was found behind a garden center, even though this spoor later turned out, sadly, to be the footprint left by a big dog. Not that it matters, since the sightings seem certain to continue, occupying a credibility notch well above UFO encounters but still below the bar of certainty. Wildlife experts respond to calls with what one fish and game biologist calls "a healthy skepticism," but there is also a growing sense among some of them that the lack of concrete, scientific proof may someday be corrected. As Kim Royer, a state wildlife biologist, told the *Bridge*, "I'm never going to say 'never' any more." Reforestation has meant the rebuilding of the deer herd and the return of moose, beaver, and wild turkey—this last is also a creature that had once vanished completely from the state but can now be spotted in abundance. One particularly airheaded specimen even took up residence on the median strip of the interstate near Randolph, where for weeks it strolled aimlessly along the shoulder, affecting an air of witless calm. Eventually it got mowed down by a passing car and became a feathered lump

decomposing on the shoulder of the road; this was a depressing sight, but it was not a sight you could have seen as
recently as fifteen years ago.

Another Vermont being, also seen routinely, is said to
live in the depths of Lake Champlain. Champ, as this creature has been nicknamed, is a benevolent and unworrisome
Loch Ness–style monster, and a minor cottage industry has
sprung up around encounter stories, explanations, and
blurry photographs—Champ, like the catamount, manifests
and then vanishes, leaving no corpse, scat, skin, or other
concrete evidence behind. Yet the people who see Champ
like to grab lapels, establish Web sites, and imagine complex
and unlikely natural histories for their chosen beast; Champ
has even been endowed with a bogus scientific name,
Champtanys, and during an irrepressible moment in the
early 1980s, both Vermont and New York moved to have
Champ declared a protected species.

Vermonters obviously like stuff like this; sometimes
there isn't much to do, and it makes our lives more interesting. But there is also a temperamental tendency to look
between the trees and conjure up mystical and valuable
beings. We speak, will, squeeze, and to some extent dream
them into being, and it's not too surprising that some of this
hard work appears in a park on a corner desperately in need
of reclamation and redemption. The push and pull between

our welcome for the wild things and our need to tame them when they appear seemed aptly acted out when, over the winter, I heard that one of the winged cat women was seen sporting a knitted woolen cap—even the wild things need some protection from the cold.

CRIME AND PUNISHMENT

O NE OF THE PLEASURES OF a small-town weekly newspaper is reading the police report, assuming the town
has its own police. Most towns don't—of the 246 cities and
towns across Vermont, only 33 have a local police department. In part, it's a money thing, and in part it's a feeling
that the police might not have all that much to do. In fact,
when the Western Rite Catholic Church began planning to
build a monastery in Craftsbury in the fall of 2000, part of
their master plan included a gift to the town of $168,000 to
finance the start-up of a town police department. The
money was intended to fund the salaries of a uniformed officer, a detective, a cruiser, and miscellaneous equipment, but
the offer was met with a quiet, questioning resistance. First,
there was no widespread feeling that anything like this was
really needed; second, and more subtly, some people in town
were uncomfortable with the idea of a bunch of unknown
newcomers using money from away to subvert municipal
and communal decisions. The third and final source of
uneasiness was that the Western Rite folks proposed that the

detective's office should be housed at the monastery, and this just didn't sit right around town.

Miffed by the cool reception, the church withdrew the offer. Afterward Archbishop Bruce J. Simpson wondered aloud, "What is there to horn in on? Is there a gold reserve or an oil well that I don't know about?" He went on to say that from then on he would be very happy to maintain a complete separation of church and state, and would be particularly glad to take full advantage of the tax-exempt status of the church and all its properties. Having gotten off on very much the wrong foot, the archbishop's relations with the town just kept unraveling like a badly made sweater; by November the group was being asked to vacate the property they were hoping to purchase because they couldn't come up with the financing, and at about the same time it emerged that one of its leading members, Alfred Deleo, was wanted on an outstanding Florida felony warrant of indecent assault on a child. The archbishop, who took the unusual position that the Florida charges were part of a conspiracy to get the church out of Vermont, gave everyone an earful. "I've lost thousands of dollars over this," he said. "I'm cutting my losses and getting out of this state. I've lived all over the world and I've never been treated like this."

So the archbishop went away mad, but the errant Deleo simply went away, saying he was off to Florida to clear his name. It won't surprise anyone to learn that he never arrived, and he was later arrested in Greensboro, Vermont, just a handful of miles from where this strange melodrama had begun. It was an absorbing spectacle, but its chief lesson, it seemed, was that when a town says they don't need a police department, they don't need a police department.

BUT BRISTOL, IT SEEMS, REALLY DOES NEED a local constabulary. In March 2000 police fielded a report of several youths frolicking around in the Brooks Pharmacy parking lot with their pants off. When they got to the scene the youths were gone, but a helpful eyewitness reported that one of the perps had last been seen wearing blue-and-white-boxer shorts. This may or may not be good information for rounding up the usual suspects, but it's an interesting choice of underwear, festive and perhaps even courageous. Courage may have been needed, since it's cold here in March, even on a good day. A few weeks later, when the warmth was apparently really returning, officers responded to a noise complaint in the recreation field, where they found twenty people sitting around a fire, six of them naked. It was a very '60s encounter and elicited a curiously '60s response. The police log reports: "Officers asked the people who were nude to get dressed and asked the remainder of the party to keep the noise down. No further complaints were received." Then, in May, police in Bristol were called to a domestic dispute between a son and his mother—a noisy and prolonged shouting match had apparently erupted over a load of laundry. The son was upset because his mother had washed an article of his clothing that had a bag of marijuana in one of the pockets, and the pot was ruined now, just ruined. After separating the two and determining what all the ruckus was about, police advised the pair that "future disputes should be calmer." Nothing was said about learning to do one's own laundry, and no charges were filed.

Within a few days the relative peace of Bristol was disrupted again by the presence of a beaver wandering down West Street. When police arrived at the scene, they found a crowd of people surrounding the animal, and when one of these idlers tried to move the beast along, the beaver went on the attack. The officers then called for some basic beaver-subduing equipment. As the animal was being lured into a cage, however, five dogs in a neighboring residence decided to get involved and broke through a Plexiglas window and ran into the crowd, snarling and nipping. Two people were bitten. When the beaver was finally secured, the officers turned their attention to the rampaging dogs, trying to snare them with collar poles, but apparently to no avail; these particular dogs were experienced with the equipment, having been snared by the constabulary at least once before. After much uproar, a relative of the dogs' owner eventually showed up and caught the excited pups. Someone found some plywood to put over the broken window. No animal restraint charges were filed, perhaps because it was hard to assign any clear-cut responsibility. The beaver was released, to everyone's relief, into Bristol Pond.

But the human and animal population of Bristol continued on its fractious and mysterious way. Later in the summer police were called in when an unnamed woman went into the hardware store, poked around for a while, and then approached the register with about $60 worth of tools that she said she wanted to return for a refund. When the items were checked against the store's computerized inventory, they were listed as still in stock; a little more checking showed the empty places on the shelves where the items had recently been. It was a weird attempt at larceny—they say a consultant is someone who borrows your watch so he can tell you what time it is, but this takes the concept several blind, or at least blurry, notches further than that. Again, no charges were filed, perhaps on the theory that the woman's technique was too iffy to qualify as an actual crime. Yet the mystifying trend continued. In August the dogs had their day again, when one particularly indignant specimen, described as "large" and "white," leaped into the side of a woman's pickup truck as she drove down West Street. The police report notes that the dog "came out of nowhere," jumping so high and with such conviction that it nearly broke the windshield, inflicting an estimated $750 in damage. The motorist was uninjured but understandably dismayed and confused. The dog, also unhurt, was seen trotting off on some inexplicable and urgent doggy errand.

It's easy to make fun, but in truth there's nothing wrong with Bristol—it's actually a decent sort of place with a reputation for having buried treasure in it. There's even a part of town called Hell's Half Acre where folks have been tunneling merrily through the solid rock for the past 200 years, looking for silver said to have been left behind by a Spaniard sometime during the colonial period. It is, of course, enchanted treasure, guarded by yet another fierce and uncontrollable dog, this time a spectral one, but I hasten to add that all this is totally normal: Every town in Vermont has at least one unhinged story attached to it, and this one happens to be Bristol's. As long as the treasure hunters keep their clothes on and buy their own shovels, everything's fine.

But crime in Vermont can take alarming and unexpected turns, and I'd be remiss if I pretended that this essentially peaceful place doesn't periodically produce some jaw-dropping violence. In August 1997 in an incident that unraveled on both sides of the Vermont–New Hampshire border, a man named Carl Drega got pulled over for a routine traffic violation and shot a New Hampshire state trooper with a semiautomatic assault rifle; when a second trooper arrived at the scene, Drega shot him, too. Drega then stole one of the cruisers and went to a downtown building where Vickie Bunell, a past select-board member and part-time judge, was working; she was scared of Drega, and when she saw him emerge from the bullet-riddled cruiser, she ran through the building telling everyone to get down, get out, and get moving. Drega came in and shot her, and then shot the editor of the local paper, who also had his office in the building, when he tried to intervene. That was four dead, and North Country police were suddenly in for a very busy day.

Drega then got back in the cruiser and drove across the border to Vermont, where he shot a game warden (who survived) and then set up an ambush by parking the stolen cruiser on a logging road with the radio blaring. Drega hid and waited to see who took the bait. Lots of law enforcement were getting involved at this point—state troopers, a police dog, the U.S. Border Patrol, and the Essex County sheriff—and before the whole business was over, more than eighty officers from pretty much every uniformed service, including the Department of Motor Vehicles, had gotten in on the act. The resulting shootout on the logging road lasted forty-five minutes, which has got to be some kind of a record around here; three more people were wounded and the gunman was finally killed.

It was a big mess, and a genuinely surprising one. Vermont and New Hampshire are two of the most peaceable kingdoms in the nation, ranked third safest and most safe, respectively—Maine wriggles in between. In a single day Drega screwed up a lot of reassuring statistics but it was more than that: He also made it much harder to sustain our fantasies about our status as decent, hardworking Yankees who settle our disputes with reasoned discourse, usually over the hot ham hash served during the lunch break at Town Meeting. As the story matured, and the background behind the incident emerged, it became clear that Drega's fury wasn't linked at all to the usual causes of murder—drugs, money, or sex—but rather to the enforcement of the local zoning ordinances. Drega had come into conflict with the town over his failure to complete a home construction project, and again after he dumped fill into a river on his property, ostensibly to control erosion. A dispute over a property assessment in 1995, which involved the judge Vickie Bunell in her role as selectwoman, escalated to the point where Drega was firing shots into the air to scare town officials off his property. Soon, he was installing motion detectors and making pipe bombs, and when law enforcement went to his house after the shooting was over, they found it was so booby-trapped, riddled with tunnels, and trip-wired with explosives that they just burned the whole business down. This last gesture smacks vaguely of revenge, but it would have been irresponsible to leave it poised to explode, since people often have a ghoulish desire to poke around scenes linked to crimes.

Incidents like this one challenged our sense of exemption, which manifests as a widespread assumption that Vermont is somehow vaccinated against human destructiveness and cruelty. This exceptionalism has been taking even more of a beating with events like the January 2000 deaths of Half and Susanne Zantop at the hands of a couple of apparently normal, pleasant teenagers from Chelsea, Vermont. This murder was so disturbing and pointless that it prompted a long meditation by the Pulitzer Prize–winning author Ron Powers in the *Atlantic*. In that essay Powers posited a kind of last-days, desperate nihilism among rural youth, driven by a mix of public policy that puts children on trial for adult crimes and, weirdly, things like the banning of skateboards in downtown Woodstock. It's a difficult argument to sustain—violent crime is actually decreasing in Vermont—but it does have a kind of creepy resonance.

The Zantop killings attracted widespread attention, in

part because the two Dartmouth professors were not your usual crime victims; their lives were understood to be more valuable because they had a nice house, good jobs, and advanced degrees. A triple homicide in Rutland, apparently drug-related, never made it onto Powers's radar screen, perhaps because it was explicable, falling well inside the drugs-money-sex triangle that drives so much violent behavior—although this, it could be argued, is just nihilism by another name. Yet the Zantop killings really were more alarming because they seemed random and, in the end, rather stupid—the two boys responsible didn't know their victims, got away with maybe $350, and had their heads full of oddball schemes about running away to Australia.

The Dartmouth murders, and to a less obvious degree the Drega spree, also point to another aspect of Yankee temperament, which is a tendency to let people pursue their own agendas and even be actively peculiar without interference. Vermonters are tolerant and mannerly: They mind their own business, they accept that not everyone's identical, and, as Russell Banks pointed out in his novel *Rule of the Bone*, they give accurate directions to homeless people wearing dreadlocks and finish up with, "Have a nice day, fellas. Which is how they talk in Vermont," says his narrator. This narrator, who may offer up a pristine if fictive example of nihilistic youth, also describes with deadpan accuracy how Burlingtonians stand in line without fidgeting, offering the world their patient and generous expressions.

Tolerance is in some ways the opposite of violence, and tolerance is a local specialty, sort of like farmstead cheese. Not long before the Zantop killings, the folks in Stowe were treated to the spectacle of a shirtless person in a full Native American headdress carrying a tomahawk around town. His appearance triggered interest but no alarm, and the buzz around the village was that he was in the area because he planned to climb Mount Mansfield to pray for world peace. Which frankly is something that can't get prayed for enough, although it did have the counter person at the Brown Bag Deli puzzled: "So why was he carrying a tomahawk?" This small psychodrama, with its overtones of curiosity and good-natured bewilderment, says a great deal about how Vermonters interpret strange behavior—they can talk about it, and they happily explore its symbolic properties, but an oddly dressed man with a weapon is accepted as part of the gestalt and mostly triggers inquiries about whether he made it all the way to the summit. Nobody saw him there, but the top of Mount Mansfield is a pretty big place. Down in the valley there was speculation that this might be the same fellow who was spotted wearing a full headdress in Morrisville earlier in the spring.

THE POLICE REPORTS IN A SMALL-TOWN NEWSPAPER often transcend the idea of news, since they also juxtapose the cultural details of a community. This probably explains why I save them and take them out periodically and coo over their contents. The Barre police log for September 25, 2000, tells me in police-speak deadpan that an individual was noted riding a bicycle down North Main Street with six new pairs of sweatpants "with tags and hangers"; later that same day a woman went into her mother's house on South Main Street and discovered "a strange young man talking to the cat," although the report is silent on what the strange young man had to say or whether the cat was holding up its end of the conversation. A month or so later—and a full year before Vermonters began to worry seriously about who might be slipping across the Canadian border—I read about Samuel Grenier of Canada, who turned up at the Derby Line customs station and began wondering aloud whether there was really a need for border inspections. To illustrate his point, he told officials he had just crossed onto American soil by coming through the woods. "After further conversation, Mr. Grenier started to leave the office, and upon being asked where he was headed, Mr. Grenier said he was 'going for a walk.' " Which he did. Soon enough he was picked up heading south on foot by a border patrol agent. Grenier then began another discussion, this one rather heated, about the oppressiveness of international boundaries. This civil disobedience gradually escalated into an uncivil tussle that ended with an application of pepper spray; he was then "handcuffed without further incident" and plonked in an American jail for processing, eventual release, and a chance to walk back across the border and make another uproar on the Canadian side. Grenier is obviously a real pain in the keister, but the story has a righteous, talkative, and inflationary innocence that makes it well worth saving.

Much has been said and speculated about the underlying causes of the low crime rates in northern New England, pretty much to no avail. Some radical thinkers seem to be advancing the idea that it's because we are all allowed to carry concealed weapons, even though most of us don't; Vermont's weapons laws reflect a hunting culture that brings with it a generic calmness about guns. The more mainstream types seem to think it's simply a characteristic of rural places, and perhaps they're right: When you look at the safest states, the list is mostly a litany of the uncrowded agricultural regions—North and South Dakota, Maine, Minnesota, Montana, Idaho, Utah, and Wyoming share the honors with New Hampshire and Vermont. But Hawaii is also in the top ten, while Nebraska isn't. Nebraska, in fact, shows up poorly against urbanized New Jersey in the rate of violent crime per

1,000 residents. The most dangerous place in the nation is Washington, DC.

So it isn't the farms, and it doesn't even seem to be the cold that keeps New England well behaved, and it seems perfectly plausible that it's what Kathleen Norris, in *Dakota: A Spiritual Geography,* calls "holy gossip." The talkative, speculative, and inquisitive dimensions of Vermont culture are reflected not just in the police blotter in the weekly paper, but also in the broad restraints operating in the community. A friend of mine, who is the publisher of a particularly enchanting small-town paper, once wrote an essay about the role of the annual town report in both fueling gossip and controlling behavior—the town report, after all, lists all the people who are delinquent on their property taxes and their water bills, and it reports their failings down to the last penny. This list is always read first, usually within nanoseconds of the report thumping through the mail slot onto the foyer floor, and for many people it is the only part of the report that seems worth perusing. Woe betide the select-board member or the community leader whose name appears there. As Kathleen Norris says, "You become public property and come to accept things that city people would consider rude." She tells a typical but revealing story of a young woman in the Dakotas using a pay phone in a cafe where she is scrutinized by the regulars. They ask, "Who are you, anyway?" It takes some prodding, but they eventually elicit her mother's maiden name. Then, "they are satisfied. They know her grandparents by reputation; good ranchers, good people." It's harder to do that here, since so many residents are immigrants, but the urge remains. When I find myself on a telephone jag, in which I spend days at a time calling up people I don't know and asking them a lot of questions, I am also asked for bona fides: "Who are you, anyway?" is rendered more obliquely in figuring out who we know in common, saying what towns we come from, and even exploring whether we once attended the same political rally. For a time I worked for a state college alumni association, which clarified my credentials enormously, since almost everyone you talk to has attended, or knows someone who attended, one of the state schools. I once rounded out a call by comparing old reunion notes with a civil engineer. "Was that the year it snowed?" "No, that was the year the old Aggies made everybody sing the alma mater." "I was there the year it snowed." "Were you the one who got stuck behind the dining hall?" "No, but I helped push. It was cold for October, as I recall."

CRIME AND PUNISHMENT SEEM inextricably linked to this need to identify, which can be vilified as sheer nosiness or celebrated for what I think it is—a desire to talk about people as if each one mattered, and to consider them one at a time. The machinery of law enforcement can be a great leveler, eroding the individual away; the response to this impersonal glaciation is the gossip, holy or unholy, that binds us together. It was exactly this impulse that drove Bruce Simpson, the Western Rite archbishop, to his distracted accusations of conspiracy—he failed to grasp that the good people of Craftsbury had to ask "Who are you?" before they could hear his suggestions or covet his money. We have a lot of faith in this process of acquaintance and understanding— as Norris says, gossip is a survival narrative, "experience translated into theology"—and it's deeply worrisome when the system fails the way it did with the murders of Half and Susanne Zantop. But it doesn't fail very often, and it didn't fail in Craftsbury, where a steady, polite, but implacable inquiry ejected a child molester from their midst. What's interesting is that that is not at all what they set out to do, but they did it anyway, and the town of Craftsbury still does not need a police department. May that continue.

How to Dress
like a Vermonter

THERE'S A GENERAL IMPRESSION in the wider world that all Vermonters buy all their clothes from the fall–winter edition of the L.L. Bean catalog, and that this some-how constitutes a fashion statement. It isn't true. Granted, it is true that some people do have clothes from L.L. Bean, but the fashion-statement part is what's misguided: There is a native costume, but it's not deliberate and it's not from a catalog. Instead, people generally buy their clothes from each other, mostly at thrift shops and yard sales, and the overall look, if that's the right word, is one of rumpled interchangeability. This means that if you live in a small town, you can follow the progress of your child's snowsuit as it works its way through a family of five at the far end of the village, until the day it appears, as if by magic, on a different child in a different family that lives two towns away. The same sartorial grammar generally holds for sweaters, fleece pullovers, jackets, hats, and windbreakers, but not for pants—pants are worn until no one else would want them.

The effect of this hand-around is curiously democratic, in that everyone seems to be dressed not just for the weather but for maximum invisibility as well. The subtle signage of fashion—the labels, lines, hues, and accessories—flares up briefly among high school students as part of the courtship display, but it doesn't seem to have much staying power beyond graduation. Students at the state colleges and the natives enrolled at the University of Vermont all seem to lapse back into wearing layers of good-enough hand-arounds, notable for coming in various sizes and in various shades of no color at all. In Burlington, where the university is, these local students endure a certain amount of condescension from the better-dressed out-of-staters, who flock to the school for its cachet and its merry environment, and are often teased or dismissed as hicks by their flashier classmates because of their drab, faded, and retro wardrobes. I've noticed, though, that by the time most of these foreigners graduate, if they ever do, they have very likely gone native themselves. Young men and women can be seen wandering on Church Street in downtown Burlington wearing brown waffle weave, work shirts laundered to extinction, and perhaps a 1960s-style sport coat in an indeterminate shade of blue, with or without tarnished metal buttons. The only way you can be sure they aren't from St. Albans or Randolph is by their use of *I* rather than *Oy* for the first-person pronoun.

But this open-ended, low-stakes attitude toward clothing can be unnerving if you aren't accustomed to it. Kiersten Conner-Sax, a downcountry freelance writer, came to Tunbridge in 1998, the year that Fred Tuttle ran for the U.S. Senate against Jack McMullen. She had come to see the spoof candidate—a retired dairy farmer in overalls and a feed cap—cast his ballot in the primary. What began as a political pilgrimage quickly morphed into an unexpected sartorial tailspin: "While I had tried not to dress conspicuously (and in Cambridge I wouldn't have stood out, in khakis and a black shirt), I felt as if I had 'outsider' stamped on my forehead," she wrote. When she encountered another reporter, she saw the same brand on him: "Although he was balding, tall, and a little stoop shouldered, he stood out the same way I did: Our clothes were too new. All the Vermonters seemed to be wearing clothes that had gotten at least five years of good use." As the story marches on, Conner-Sax's clothing anxiety gradually becomes its central theme: "The residents of Tunbridge looked at us as if we were invading marauders," she wrote. "It felt strange to see myself through their eyes, lumped in with the plastic-coated television reporters, a flatlander with a notebook. No, I wanted to say, I'm not sure my car will make it back to Massachusetts, and I can't raise my arms because the air conditioning's broken and I seem to have sweated through this silk shirt, which has a torn collar, anyway."

Conner-Sax's cascade of self-consciousness was entirely self-generated and almost certainly well below the radar of the people of Tunbridge, who generally don't notice what anybody is wearing unless it's Halloween and definitely a costume, which means you are supposed to guess who's inside. They certainly don't notice, as Conner-Sax did, that the Tunbridge town clerk was wearing "a purple silk blouse over a turtleneck and thick pearls." This mildly astonishing ensemble was perhaps a variation on what this particular town clerk wore to work every day—when nobody cares, a lot of individual quirkiness percolates through—or perhaps, because of the media interest in the Fred Tuttle story, she put on the blouse and the pearls because she was almost sure to get her picture taken. Either way, I'm quite sure that Conner-Sax was overstating when she wrote that the clerk "eyed me with a look I can only describe as distrust," since in my experience most town clerks are as nice as pie.

What's notable about this encounter is that the reporter interpreted the Vermont fashion difference as hostile when I doubt that it was—Vermonters can be hostile, but it doesn't usually erupt over clothes. Mess with their guns, their kids, or the tubing that runs through the woods and brings the sap to the sugarhouse and there will probably be hell to pay, but I've never met a Vermonter who cared what anybody, anywhere had on. This became particularly notice-able when I moved to the capital city of Montpelier. Because it's the seat of the government and the legislature, there are people in Montpelier who iron their clothes and wear things that match and own actual neckties. They flicker on the sidewalks like sleek, polished birds; the sur-faces of their clothes have a smoothness and a sheen that makes them seem vaguely metallic. Women swish by and you can actually hear that they are wearing panty hose from the delicate friction of thread against thread; their shoes don't have much in the way of laces or waterproofing. But here's the thing: Nobody notices. There's no extra defer-ence offered to these smartly dressed lawmakers and lobby-ists, and they don't seem to expect deference, either. They are wearing a uniform, not making a social or economic utterance; it's as if they were firemen or maybe game war-dens. And because Vermont has a true citizen legislature—this is shorthand for saying they get paid squat and put in a lot of hours—there's a generic sense that having to get dressed up for work is just part of the hardship, like circling the block for parking and eating lunch standing up. And it remains a hardship. When U.S. senator Patrick Leahy engaged in an online chat with the Mount Holly third grade, a child named Samantha asked him, "When you go to work, do you have to dress up?" He replied, "I have to

wear a suit and tie at work. I enjoy getting home in the evening and changing into a sweatshirt and jeans." He wasn't just being pleasantly accessible and downscale—when Pat Leahy comes home, he can be spotted wearing pretty much what I'm wearing right now, which is exactly what I wore yesterday, except this set is clean.

THE PROBLEM OF CLOTHING IN VERMONT has mainly been discussed when no clothes were in the offing. This same Patrick Leahy, back when he was the state's attorney for Chittenden County, once wrote the quintessential position paper on skinny-dipping in the form of a memo to the various boys in blue. It was 1971, and the back-to-the-land folks, who saw Vermont as a kind of Eden, were not always as discreet as they could have been in their clothing-optional practices, resulting in some phone calls to local and state police. The hippie invasion of the '60s and '70s was not met with universal enthusiasm, and some of these complaints were probably less about clothing and more about feeling put upon, but whatever the trigger it must be said that the future senator rose to the occasion. Whether you like his politics or not, Leahy has always been marked by a typical Vermonter's willingness to be thorough, fair, and happily absorbed by the resolution of issues that do not really matter. He even proves that, in some cases, the less it matters, the better. Leahy said:

> A number of law-enforcement agencies have asked this office for advice in view of the revival of the time-honored practice of unclothed swimming known colloquially as "skinny-dipping." I was originally disinclined to slow the crime-fighting operation of the Chittenden County State's Attorney's Office long enough to issue a memorandum of such minuscule moment.
>
> However, I have been reminded that in the past the plethora of Paper from this office has included such legal landmarks as my position on the use of sparklers on the Fourth of July (a position hedged with great patriotic fervor) and the validity of upside-down license plates (complete with instructions on how to determine the sobriety of the operator at the time he attached the plate).
>
> With such powerful precedents in mind, I ensconced myself at my family's summer farm near Montpelier during the Fourth of July Weekend and researched the issue. I began by reviewing the old Norman Rockwell paintings, thoughtfully resurrected by the ACLU, showing such activities taking place allegedly in Vermont (along this line I was unable either to confirm or refute the persistent rumor that Vermont's number one politician, Calvin Coolidge, had also engaged in such activity within the borders of this State while subject to Vermont's laws).

I have also discussed—after grants of immunity—experiences of this nature enjoyed by some of Vermont's prosecutors, judges, law-enforcement officers, and sailboat operators. After checking the Statute of Limitations, I have even reviewed past histories with some of my contemporaries during my teenage years in Montpelier. Also, each member of my office offered to investigate this matter in an undercover manner (so to speak).

It appears that most Vermonters I've talked to have engaged in such scandalous activity at some time in their life (with the exception of a couple I didn't believe who claimed to have done so in May in Vermont). Times, however, do change. Today such things are apparently allowable in most movies, on Canadian Television, in the *National Geographic* and *Life* magazine, but by no means in the pristine rivers and streams of Vermont. Therefore, to guide any law-enforcement officer so lacking in other criminal matters to investigate, so as to have time to investigate this currently popular subject of skinny-dipping, I offer, in all seriousness, the following guidelines:

In public areas (e.g. North Beach in Burlington) and semi-public areas: Nude bathing is not acceptable. In such instances, the officer receiving the complaint should order the person to dress. Failure to stay clothed should result in a summons to Court.

On private land out of view of the public: The State has no legitimate interest and swimmers should be left alone.

In secluded areas sometimes publicly used (e.g. rivers, swimming holes, etc.): If no member of the public present is offended, no disorderly conduct has taken place. If members of the public (e.g. families wishing to use the swimming area) complain, then proceed as in No. 1 above.

Everything about this memorandum, from the capitalization of *Paper* to the business about the upside-down license plates to the discursive parentheses, carries a kind of essential distractibility, a be-here-now willingness to mess around with details and have some fun. It probably says something fairly concrete about why the author went on to become a senator. But it's also serious: As far as I can tell, this policy is still more or less intact, not because it's funny but because it's culturally correct. There have been (and will be again) periodic uproars about naked people—an antinudity ordinance passed by the town of Wilmington in 2002 disrupted a long history of sunning in the buff on the ledges at Harriman Reservoir but was overturned on a second vote in 2003. Also in 2002, White River Junction citizens debated whether they needed an ordinance to address the unexpected eruption of naked people in the form of nude dancing in the White River Amusement Pub, which had begun as a karaoke club and was apparently skidding badly downhill. Weirdly, the biggest single concern during the discussion in White River was whether adopting nudity regulations might somehow interfere with nudity, which it obviously would. The consensus was that, from a privacy, civil liberties, and happiness-quotient standpoint, this would be a bad thing. During the discussion, which was lively, Pastor Jim Olsen of the Hartford United Church of Christ revealed that he himself had been skinny-dipping in the Connecticut River just in the past couple of weeks. "On account of the warm weather," he explained. Everybody found this kind of funny, but mostly it proved a point.

Pastor Jim aside, Vermont isn't really all that clothing-optional because most of the time it's too cold—there is, as one saying goes, ten months of winter and two months of damned poor sledding. Yet even cold-weather clothing behavior proceeds on a kind of automatic pilot. In 1992 a couple of researchers named Zbikowski and Loker did a study of the differences in the bedtime clothing practices of Floridians and Vermonters and discovered that the people in Florida actually reported wearing more clothes—hats, socks, slippers, coats, pajamas, and other heat-retention devices— than Vermonters did and were also significantly more likely to pile on the quilts and electric blankets and take a heating pad with them to bed. This is a strange finding, since the study also showed that Vermonters know a lot more about hypothermia and its dangers. The researchers were naturally a little puzzled, and decided, as always, that more research was necessary, but I think I can save them the money and the trouble. The obvious explanation is that the Vermonters wore plenty of clothes, but they didn't remember putting them on. It's an easy kind of forgetting to do when you live here. During a recent cold spell, when it plummeted to the minus twenties at night and made it up to zero during the sunny part of the day, I went to the local gym to swim some laps. When I got there, I found that my usual three or four layers had inexplicably jumped to seven—underneath the usual parka, tweed jacket, sweater, and turtleneck there was an olive sweatshirt, a tan jersey with long sleeves, and a tatty T-shirt that said SAN DIEGO on the front. This sartorial archaeology genuinely surprised me, since I didn't know they were there. I was also startled because none of these clothes looked particularly familiar. I am beginning to think everyone in the state owns an olive sweatshirt that came from nobody-knows-where.

I BRING THIS UP BECAUSE I'm convinced that, when clothes don't matter, human attention gets freed up for other things—like skinny-dipping, maybe, but other essential things as well. I don't think it's an accident, for example, that each time I have run into Stephen Huneck he has worn what appears to be the same flannel shirt. It's either brown or dull blue or a vague, neutral green—I can't remember and I bet neither can he. Like Studs Terkel, who owns a dozen copies of exactly the same ensemble, Huneck exerts the artists' prerogative of wearing what amounts to nothing at all—this isn't clothing-optional so much as it is clothing without traction for the memory. This is as it should be. What's really memorable about Huneck is that he talks a lot and feels strongly about what he's saying. In 1994 he fell down a flight of stairs, went into a coma, and developed something called adult respiratory distress syndrome. This is a bad thing to have, and nobody was hopeful about his recovery except Huneck and his wife, Gwen. After two months Huneck somehow reemerged and began relearning his life—he started from zero with handling spoons and pencils and moved on to writing his name. Huneck's recovery was slow but illuminating; he says that it made him understand that we don't dwell long enough, or often enough, on the things that really matter. "What matters," he says, "is love. There isn't anything else. People fear death because they don't want to lose things, but the plain truth is that they will lose things. You can't let that get in the way. You have to love."

Talking to Stephen Huneck means that your ears are lifted for the sound of the platitude alert, which is a loud, steady beeping that carries well in the North Country. For various reasons the alarm does not sound. There are unfashionable and irony-free forces at work here. First, Huneck was a practicing and widely admired artist before his illness, and afterwards he put his artistry on the line. He got a kind of religion, built around an uncompromised and radiant passion for love, and more specifically for the love between animals and humans, and it was this experience that drove him to build the Dog Chapel, up on Dog Mountain, just east of St. Johnsbury. This building is a New England–style Greek Revival church with tall double doors and stained-glass windows. Or at least that's what it looks like. For a moment, when you approach it, there is apparently nothing new, just another house of worship with another spire pointing endlessly at the sky. And because it looks like what we half expect to see, there's a long moment when we do not really see it, and do not notice that it is too small to be true, and too carefully made to be false. Its perfection of detail and proportion offers a strange, near-perfect mix of joy and stubbornness; its handcraftiness is a kind of subverted, trompe l'oeil icon that plays on our expectations. The sign in the dooryard says WELCOME. ALL CREEDS, ALL BREEDS. NO DOGMAS ALLOWED.

The Dog Chapel took four years to build, and when you go in you can see why. All of Huneck's work—chiefly prints, sculpture, and furniture—is careful and lavish, but this small building on a hillside may be the best example of his almost obsessive craftsmanship. Or, if not the best, it's certainly the biggest, and Huneck freely acknowledges that the Dog Chapel is an appropriation: "I want people to see something they think they know about." He then uses that knowledge to surprise the viewer and to celebrate our lives with our animals. And because this is a chapel, the particular focus is on the part of life that comes after the animal's life has ended.

As you step inside you are greeted by several things, but the anchor object in the foyer is a life-sized black Labrador carved from wood with gilded wings. The Lab's paws are stretched forward in flight and anticipation, so that the creature sails, sort of like Superman, toward heaven. It's strange and schmaltzy, but there's no question it's serious: Huneck's dogs are all suffused with a deep dogginess, with their thick necks and their nobly lifted chins and their calm expressions, and the weird camp of the sculpture is one thing, but not the important thing, about it. Moving on and in, into the chapel proper, this collision of merriment and seriousness deepens. There are stained-glass windows with dogs where the saints would be, and there is a carved English spaniel in the place normally reserved for an altar. Sweet music plays; the hymnals in the pews are copies of Huneck's picture book, SALLY GOES TO THE BEACH. Sally is a dog.

Huneck links the Dog Chapel with his desire, in all his

work, to name the important things and confront our losses. "Dogs teach us how to love," he says. "Dogs also die, and people who have lost their dogs truly suffer." He points out that there is no adequate mechanism to honor those deaths, and the resulting grief can be carried as an inner wound for decades. "The purity of a dog's love is transforming, and I want the Dog Chapel to address that."

He gets his wish. The stained-glass windows evoke, almost relentlessly, the canine behavior we cherish. He shows us play, loyalty, friendship, and devotion; the pew seats and backs are held in place by carved dogs in the "sit" position, perhaps waiting patiently for masters who have stepped around the corner for the morning paper. The tall candles, the overtly religious spaces, all work to elevate the place of dogs from the cold kennel to the hot, gushing heart, where, in Huneck's universe, they perform small but continuous miracles.

THE IDEA THAT THE DOG–HUMAN BOND is sacred has deep roots in Western culture, but it has always been a rather mournful relationship—we tend to outlive our canine companions. Old age, it has been observed, is that moment when you realize you won't have time to own all the dogs you wanted to, and no less a writer than Kipling suffered openly in his "Power of the Dog" when he said, "Brothers and sisters, I bid you beware / Of giving your heart to a dog to tear." The Dog Chapel emerges from this tradition with an almost shameless flourish, making a powerful appeal to our senses and to our sense of humor: A pooch with a halo is both funny and touching, silly but somehow accurate. Huneck knows that he walks a fine line between what works and what is just a little too much, and he achieves balance by trusting his impulses. And by trusting his five dogs, which he observes closely. "Dogs teach us how to trust, how to have honor, how to play," he says, and the desire to build the chapel, once it entered his mind, seemed to get stuck there. "The more I thought about it," he says in the chapel mission statement, "the more I realized it was something I simply had to do."

As impulses go, this one was unusually expensive. Huneck estimates he spent about $175,000 building it and concedes that it took up a big chunk of time and money he didn't actually have. Even with his success—Huneck has a main gallery in Woodstock, Vermont, a gallery here on Dog Mountain, and work featured in the permanent collections of the Smithsonian, the Museum of American Folk Art, and the Contemporary Museum of Art in Sydney, Australia—he's still an artist, a profession where money is thin on the ground. But he didn't waver: "I wanted this. This is what time and money are for. I would rather have a Dog Chapel than a pile of stocks any day."

This fearlessness—about money, about schmaltz, about his

own vulnerability—is what marks Stephen Huneck's work. By addressing the clean, final, and unquestioning love between a dog and a human, he applies a kind of lever and pries the shell around love apart; he wants us to feel more love, and to get the love we are capable of right out into the open. And, frankly, it works. If you ever had a dog that lifted your heart, protected your interests, and accompanied you through time, then the Dog Chapel's wall of remembrance, complete with blurry photos and fond good-byes, is perfectly contrived to make you revisit that relationship. Visitors can post their pet pictures and stories here, and the wall is full—whatever Huneck is up to, and whatever might be said about it, it hits a high, trembling, emotional note with visitors. The doggy pictures have a melancholy that is awkwardly lovely; the accompanying messages, couched in what ought to be the least interesting language imaginable, read as rags of raw, authentic feeling. "I miss you," says one. "Life goes on," says another, "but it won't be as interesting." "My first dog," says a third. "I will love you forever."

The Dog Chapel is about dogs, but no domestic animal is excluded; the wall of remembrance offers up a range of other creatures, including a double-ended, rather enigmatic guinea pig that looks exactly like a mop. And several cats—it's hard not to notice that there's a difference in tone to these feline farewell messages. A smiling orange tabby sits on a doorstep over the epitaph, "Are you happy in hell?" Another cat message says, "James, I forgive you, and I hope you have found peace." There's a truthfulness here, and support for Roy Blount's observation in the *Atlantic* that dogs come when they are called, but cats take a message and get back to you. Seen from a cynical distance, these messages might seem a little shop-worn, but context, in the end, is everything. The wall is not for wailing so much as for quiet sniffling, and for expressing the complexities of uncomplicated love. And this context proves, far better than the tears in my own eyes, that the Dog Chapel does what it sets out to do—it does the heavy lifting of grief and it clears the mind of everything except the happiness only a dog can bring.

What saves the Dog Chapel from sappiness is its headlong conviction and Huneck's own artistry—it's impossible to talk about the project without mentioning its narrative precision. Huneck's dogs chase balls, eat things they shouldn't, lick their genitals, and sneeze; he evokes the well-fed, tubular bodies of dogs that lead fortunate lives. The folksiness of these works is actually a little deceptive, since their intent is the opposite of easy and naive, and the cumulative impact of these images is surprisingly sophisticated and surprisingly uncalculated—they work for the viewer because they are part of a belief system.

"I never learned, growing up, that touch was a way of expressing affection," Huneck explains. "It was painful, some-thing to be avoided." Yet his work is almost aggressively tactile, with its careful carving and its pervasive sense of having been handled by its maker; the craftsmanship becomes a kind of redemption, arrived at the hard way. Touch matters. One of Huneck's images is of his Labrador, Molly, almost completely obscured by human hands that touch her face and head reverently; it's a pleasing and ambiguous image that tells us everything we need to know about stroking and reciprocity.

I have to ask Huneck if he's worried that he's gotten artistically stuck. Do you ever want to move on to rocket ships or insects? "Actually, I have done rocket ships and insects," he says, "and I just finished a full-sized nun." Much of his work is done on commission and rests in private collections, and his client list includes Madeline Kunin, Vermont's governor from 1985 to 1991, and Pat Leahy, the congressman who keeps reappearing in this chapter like a theme in a minor key. But Huneck's appeal isn't just local: His work is also owned by folks from away, like Maria Shriver. "I don't think I'm stuck," he says, "but this is something I want to keep coming back to. And I have to be honest—I don't really care what other people think.

"When I was sick, while I was recovering, the doctors told me that people who have been in prolonged comas like I had been often become mentally unstable. They said I could expect to have psychotic symptoms. I could possibly become paranoid, afraid and suspicious of everything. But the opposite happened—I lost my fears, and I gained an appreciation of life's basic things. I let that appreciation be how I live my life and do my work."

It's time for true confessions—I went to high school with Stephen Huneck and can conjure, with surprising vividness, a distant and preoccupied upperclassman who haunted the art department, just as I did. These happy spatial accidents happen all the time in the cramped world of New England, and one result of this overcrowding is that I can confirm that the artist then and the artist now really are two radically different people. In 1965 Huneck was inward and impenetrably silent; now his heart is often on his sleeve and he won't shut up. I like the late-model Huneck better than the earlier one, but I also think, with some sadness, that serious illness is a miserable way to buff up one's artistic credentials. I'm not saying it didn't work or wasn't worth it; it just seems expensive. But life, as Huneck tells me, is expensive. Love cripples and distorts us if we can't name it, feel it, and suffer when love is over.

One memorable thing we had in common back then was a teacher who alternately inspired and exasperated, and who once insisted, rather maniacally, that we spend several weeks building a henhouse full of papier-mâché chickens and plaster eggs. He made us play with blocks and throw our sculptures out the window, insisting that the impact with the sidewalk would make them much more interesting; he pushed us, annoyed us, and teased us relentlessly, and he was probably the reason both Huneck and I continued on to different art schools. "He was complicated and unhappy," Huneck tells me, and he goes on to disclose some of the details of our teacher's messy private life and truly bizarre domestic arrangements. I am not all that surprised, but I am surprised that Huneck had access, even then, to the driving miseries that defined and sometimes distorted other people's lives. How did he know? I remember only an unpredictable and merry little man who often gave me a lift to school in the mornings in his pale green Mustang; during the ride in he would suck down cigarettes and needle me about my clothes—I was, back then, already mor-phing into the sort of person who could not be bothered. But this same eccentric and surprisingly able teacher also consented to write me a lengthy and glowing recommendation to Pratt Institute. After I was accepted, he offered his loud congratula-tions but immediately went on to warn me: "You won't last. You'll find something easier." He was right.

I have to ask Huneck if it worries him that the chapel stirs up so many strong feelings, and whether he is encouraging people to view their animals as fuzzy children. "No," he says. "Love is love." But what, I ask, about the moral dangers of anthropomorphism? "I think that's intellectual bullshit," he replies. "It comes back to love, which is always in too short supply." He's roughing me up a little—I can tell he's tired of this kind of question—but it's actually fun to be on the receiving end, and it's fun to find myself, later, agreeing with him. Yes, I once had a dog, and I loved him with exactly the kind of clarity that Huneck exposes, and for almost a year after he died I could still hear the tap of his toenails on the wood floor of the hall; I once even saw him romping toward me across a frozen pasture with something illegal, dead, and smelly in his big wet mouth. These visitations made me happy, like home movies from a better time, but that happiness is not the point, or at least not the whole point. What I'd also felt—vacuous glee aside—was a kind of nakedness, an unexpected exposure to the force of my own needs and wishes, which were so fierce that they willed a dead dog back into being. It was craven, needy, childish, self-serving, and, I think, completely necessary. It proved, among other things, that I was capable of something dangerously close to a different kind of skinny-dipping, of letting the warm water of old grief close over my head. For Huneck this immersion is entirely the point, and Huneck's flying dog has somehow won me over—mostly because it does fly, but also because it is the kind of dog that could just as easily go swimming and emerge from the pond wearing frog cologne. We could take a dip together, and I doubt that anyone would care or criticize. Like the memo says, the state has no interest and swimmers should be left alone.

THE ART CAPITAL
OF THE WORLD

A WHILE BACK THERE WAS A STORY in the paper about how many artists lived in Vermont, and it seemed to be saying that the incidence of artiness was very high here, running second only to New Mexico. This surprised me until I saw that this high ranking was based on percentage of the population—when you only have 600,000 people, you can see a pretty decent uptick in the arty quotient when Circus Smirkus, a seasonal clown-and-juggler incubator up in Hardwick, is in session, or when the annual uproar of the Bread Loaf Writers' Conference is in full swing. Still, the news item interested me and seemed like a good excuse to waste an entire day looking at occupational reports and making phone calls. I wanted to know: How are artists found, named, and counted?

Apparently, it's a bit like counting fish. Artists are a variable, silent, and moving target in terms of the census, since there's no unambiguous census category that rounds up writers, actors, dancers, painters, sculptors, and musicians and puts them all in the same big pile. And even if the census tried to do that, there would still be a miscount, because artists are also like frost heaves—they come and go, cluster and disperse, and change with the weather. Worse, many of their efforts are hard to categorize. What's the status of the person who lives on Route 2, just outside Richmond, who has collected dozens of stainless-steel milk cans and used them to fill up the entire front lawn with impromptu modular sculpture? Who painted the laughing angel on the barn on Route 12 in Roxbury? How do we classify all the mailboxes transformed into dogs, ears of corn, Uncle Sam, insects, automobiles, and Holsteins? Poets are even more difficult, since their work percolates to the surface only under certain conditions. As a practical matter, being a poet is a lot like having some minor chronic illness along the lines of hay fever or restless leg syndrome—it afflicts the victim but is largely invisible to others. A poet looks like a dentist or a mail carrier with a lot on her mind. In fact, a poet often *is* a dentist or a mail carrier with a lot on her mind.

The Vermont Arts Council lists 423 practicing artists in its 2003 directory. Weirdly, despite having received a council grant to write this book, I am not listed there, and neither are the many regional authors, locally famous, or the impressive roster of Vermont writers with national reputations—David Mamet, Grace Paley, Jamaica Kincaid, Julie Alvarez, John Irving, Howard Frank Mosher, Jeffrey Lent,

Archer Mayor, Chris Bohjalian, Jay Parini, John Elder, and Annie Proulx before she decamped to Wyoming or wherever it was she went. And others—I have a bad memory for names. There are also more musicians in Vermont than you can shake a stick at. The state is a stronghold of bluegrass, Celtic, classical, jazz, French Canadian, and the grab-bag kitchen music that arises noisily and without preamble in rural places everywhere—and yet the register lists thirty active musicians statewide. That's kind of pathetic, but it mostly proves my point: You can't count artists the way you can count fence posts or highway miles.

You can make an inventory of artistic institutions and enterprises—museums, galleries, community and professional theaters, and historical displays—and I managed to find 311 of these without trying very hard. That's about one establishment for every 1,929 people, or, to change the terms a bit, 5.18 places of artistic and cultural amusement for every 10,000 people. Santa Fe, New Mexico, claims 3.22—admittedly, our weather is worse, but it looks like we've got no lines, no waiting. In the Barre-Montpelier area, where I live, there are three historical societies, four museums, twelve galleries, two theaters—one professional and one community—a music school, and the headquarters of the Vermont Philharmonic. Barre and Montpelier, combined, have a population of about 18,000 people, which gives us a yield of 12.7

art shops per 10,000 people. These are dumb numbers and I know it, since the true cultural vivacity of a place can't be captured by this kind of quantification, but if Vermont wanted to make the claim that it's the art capital of the nation and perhaps the world, we might actually get away with it.

Nobody's trying, but in February 2003 a South Burlington business owner named Bill Schubart told a gathering of the chamber of commerce that Vermont ought to accentuate this particular positive by deliberately luring oddball people and enterprises to the state. Our strongest niche, he said, has generally proved to be along the lines of stuffed bears and gourmet ice cream, so why not face facts and seek out small, wacko businesses that will thrive in Vermont's atmosphere of tolerance and good cheer? He even proposed that we think about following in the footsteps of Ireland and make artistic earnings tax-free. This is a very entertaining idea, and nowhere near as risky as it sounds. Schubart didn't say—but I will—that an exemption like this won't have much impact on the state treasury. According to the National Endowment for the Arts, artists are unusually well educated and often highly committed to their craft, but they make lousy money. Among unemployed musicians, which is most musicians, one in eight was out of work for two to five years at a stretch. Seventy to 90 percent of all creative writers work a second job, often teaching. The NEA reported, with an almost audible sigh, that "without income from their second or multiple jobs, a majority of authors would be classified as poor."

In general, having a lot of poor people around is not all that good for the economy, but artists may be an exception. Richard Florida, who has made a splash for himself by talking about what he calls the "creative class," points out that creative people grow up "feeling like outsiders, different in some way from their classmates." When they go looking for a place to live, they don't care much for the things that many cities heavily invest in, like swanky malls or football stadiums or a glittering and convenient airport. What they look for instead is a welcome sign—NON-STANDARD PEOPLE WELCOME HERE—and for signals that the new place will engage and stimulate. Florida has focused his attention on cities like Austin, Chapel Hill, and Boston, but rural places have long been a refuge for the square pegs of this world. Vermont, with its gay-rights legislation, its accessible and sometimes unhinged politics, and its cultural tendency to place a high value on individuals, could be called a billboard message to the creative class, except we don't have billboards here. We don't like them. Billboards are tacky.

YOU CAN'T THROW A GRANOLA BAR in Vermont without having it bounce off the head of someone with artistic ambitions, even if those ambitions are private and modest. And in some ways the small efforts, done without pyrotechnics or an eye for glory, are the most interesting. For example, it's hard not to think of Harry Barber when confronted with the specter of the rural, part-time, passionate, and uncompensated creator. It can certainly be argued, perhaps cogently, that what Barber made was not really art, but I'm not going to do that. He made what he thought was art, and right now that's good enough for me.

Barber came to Vermont from Switzerland in the 1920s, leaving behind him a disrupted and war-scarred Europe, and ended up on the open, sunny shores of South Hero, which is the southernmost of the islands in Lake Champlain. He was the son of a stonemason, and brought with him what looks like a natural passion for lofty medieval architecture. This passion may also have been bolstered by place: These islands, which are surprisingly flat by Vermont standards, have a weird and distant beauty. They float apart, nearly treeless, with long water vistas and outcroppings of ancient fossils and a thick yellow silence that permeates everything, despite the endless raking of the air. It's always windy on the islands, but it's also densely still—a contradiction that I can't explain except to say there is a monastic, plainsong quality to the islands, so firmly established that it even comes with a particular color. The islands, even in high summer, have an undertone of dried sunflowers, golden grass, and new pumpkins.

Against this background of apartness and thanksgiving, Barber collected stones from the beaches and used them to build dozens of detailed, perfectly scaled small castles, a project that consumed most of his leisure time and ended with his death in 1960. In the cluster of buildings that makes up the village of South Hero, on a lawn across from the school, is one of the surviving examples. Granted, it's small for a castle—it stands only about four feet high—but it comes complete with towers, a keep, a moat, and a chivalrous expression. It features arched windows, high walks, turrets, and platforms from which boiling oil can be poured onto the heads of tiny marauding enemies, and it's all built out of gray pebbles of remarkably even size and consistency. "Harry Barber liked stone," says Janice Lavallee, the castle's owner, "but it's probably a little more complicated than that."

Lavallee takes me on a tour of the details: the cloister walk, the winding stairs between the floors, the high gable with the round window that once held a tiny clock. "A pocket watch, probably," she says; this tower clock is now long gone. So are the glass windows and the wooden doors that once hung on delicate metal hinges; Lavallee keeps these tiny, damaged treasures in a kitchen drawer for future restoration. The castle even has its own plumbing—a modest arrangement of pipes to keep the moat filled, though today the moat is dry. "It's wired, too," she says, pointing at the old knob-and-tube that winds through the structure. "Harry's original idea was that the interior would light up at night, as if someone were really living there."

Obviously these structures weren't built to evoke some shorthand idea of castle. They were instead built from the inside out, full of details you can't see, as if Barber were intent on developing legitimate housing for the Little People. You see something of the same urge operating among model-railroad buffs, who lavish infinite care on the landscape and buildings, but the Barber castles—the ones that have survived—are both more primitive and more packed with conviction. His work plays on more than just our human delight in sudden changes of scale. Barber also played on, and with, our secret childhood conviction that all the interesting things happen while we are not looking, and that there is a parallel, smaller world that is fully populated and needs decent lighting.

THE BOUNDARY BETWEEN HANDMADE backyard art and hand-made backyard kitsch has always been permeable. The Watts Tower in Los Angeles, begun in the '20s by an Italian American tile setter, sits on the decidedly arty end, while the more prosaic painted rock garden, complete with the gazing globe and the plaster bunnies, sits lumpishly on the other.

The work of Harry Barber lies somewhere in between, but it's hard to be sure whether this castle merely straddles the line or actually defines it. The castle is a serious piece of whimsy, a minor and merry masterpiece, but it's also inward and, despite its charm, a little disconcerting, the work of a man who was lavishly romantic and perhaps a little homesick.

Lavallee and I begin the short tour of the surviving Barber castles that can be seen from the road, and our first stop is at the Hemingway place. Bob Hemingway is up on a ladder, painting along the eaves, when we cross the lawn to ask permission to take a close look at his sample of Barber architecture. He gives it graciously, but he's definitely not coming down—if you want to ask questions, you get to squint and holler. He remembers Harry Barber as a coworker and friend; he tells us from his lofty perch that his personal castle was moved to his house from the lawn of the South Hero Inn.

"Was it a big deal to move it?"

"Nope. Came apart in sections, nice as you please."

"How come you wanted it?"

"Well," he explains without explaining, "I was raising pigs. I hauled the garbage one summer from the inn to feed them, and I got them to give me that castle in exchange."

"How well did you know Harry?"

"Pretty well, I'd guess."

"Did you ever ask him why he built the castles?"

"Nope."

"Did he ever tell you why?"

"Nope."

"What was Harry like?"

"Harry? Harry was a real nice man."

Hemingway dips his brush and goes back to something useful; the interview is over.

THE MYSTERY OF HARRY BARBER lies not in his person—he worked locally as a caretaker, a gardener, and a farm laborer—but in his output. The castles would be easy to dismiss as mere oddities but for their sheer abundance and their expectant expressions—they seem, despite their decay, to obstinately expect a tenant to be moving in the following day. Barber's widow remembers one tiny house he built, now gone, that was in move-in condition right down to the curtains. He came home every day with rocks in his pocket, culled from the beaches and quarries, and it seems that collecting and sorting the stones was one of his steady, overriding occupations. He picked out his stones with specific projects in mind, and then spent the long and relatively inactive Vermont winters building the castles in sections in his workshop. One castle is a pearly pink; another is white;

others are various shades of gray. The castle shapes also vary—some are slender, shapely homes for Tinkerbell, while others are muscular and military. One surviving example sits at the water's edge and fixes its steady gaze on the New York shoreline. It has a dungeon and it frowns and it clearly means business, and acts as a sentinel against any questionable doings across the bay.

It could be that these confections say something about what life was like before television, but it may say even more about part-time artists and how they operate. Whatever you make of Barber's castles, he made as much as he could of them, and they show that Barber built like a true architect. The castles have not just floors but floor plans; rooms flow from one to the other; stairs operate between the levels, often curve, and have windows to light them. Along a high walkway there are tiny metal chains to prevent the imaginary occupants from plummeting to their imaginary deaths on the rocks below.

I ask Lavallee, who rides shotgun on a tour of Harry's castles, what she thinks Harry was up to—she lives daily with a castle and might have some insights. "I think Harry Barber was a real, incurable romantic," she says. "He wanted to make things by hand, in his own way. I think about all the glass windows and all the little doors—all the details—and I just think he wanted people's lives to be lovely, to have a mystery."

Loveliness and mystery can be expensive, though; in the end, the pursuit of these two pleasures seem to have cost Harry Barber more than he could afford. It's said that Barber committed suicide, which is a strange way to end a life that was caught up in apparently endless acts of creation. The story goes that Barber was trying to get Electra Havemeyer Webb, the wealthy patroness behind the Shelburne Museum, interested in his work—Webb's lifelong mission was to scoop up American folk art and place it on a pedestal of artistic legitimacy. It's murky what actually happened between them, but the outcome was that, despite Barber's passion, his work was not going to be given a place in the pantheon that Webb was building. Webb may have decided that Barber's work was too kitschy or maybe not kitschy enough, but it was in this context that Barber ended his life. Whether there was any cause and effect operating, or whether this was merely the moment when melancholy overcame romanticism, is just plain unknown.

Over time, much of Barber's work has quietly crumbled away—even though these Camelots were built with care and workmanship, nothing that lives outdoors year-round in Vermont has permanence as a working option. As Lavallee and I wrap up our castle itinerary, I can't decide if this troubles me or not. There is something curiously pleasing about the idea of these tiny, interesting castles slowly melting in the golden light into tiny, interesting ruins. What does trouble me is the suicide—it seems utterly unnecessary—and as I begin the long drive home, this becomes the nagging detail that changes these charming artifacts. They seem less sunny and more ambiguous.

But good art, in some final way, is always rooted in discomfort or at least in change, and I am reminded of this as I pass through some unnamed crossroad somewhere north of Burlington. I have to slow down to witness the spectacle of a middle-age woman intently playing a piano in front of a farmhouse in the spring twilight. Surrounded by battered dressers and picture frames and glassware, she pounds away happily and waves back at me as I go by. A piece of cardboard, taped to the piano, says MOVING SALE in rough capital letters, and for a pleasurably confusing moment I have no idea what the sign refers to. When I do figure it out, I want this woman to keep her piano. Her joy in the music is obvious and sustaining. Life is short and often hard, but art is long. As I pass the house, I realize that I like living in a place where, like Harry Barber, we can practice the arts out on the lawn.

THE DAY AFTER
MUD SEASON

THERE COMES A DAY TOWARD THE END of mud season—a period called "spring" in the rest of the country—when the yeasty, wet-dirt smell, sort of like a soggy sponge, suddenly widens one warm afternoon to include the reek of skunk and the sudsy scent of budding forsythia. It's a moment dear to the hearts of Vermonters. Even though there is no visible change—the landscape is still brown and the water is still rising in the basement—there is a difference. Mud season is starting to yield and it is safe to come out, blinking and unbundled, wearing the same exact clothes you wore inside. This a daring gesture, like the first venture into the hallway after a long illness, and there is something fragile and a little unhinged about it. In the capital, I have seen grown men sitting down on the sidewalk to read the newspaper, as if overcome by mysterious fumes; others lean dangerously far out of windows. Others put on shorts and tank tops, even if it's still in the fifties, even if there's a brisk southerly breeze. They look wan and hopeful and poke their

Hacky Sacks dimly; the knitted balls dribble in tiny, lopsided arcs, like frogs with injured legs. It's tentative at first, but the tiny pivot between mud and summer is here.

With the advent of the growing season comes an operational change in the action of sunlight. I've never heard a reasonable explanation for this, but there really are regional differences in how light travels from the star to the planet. You never see, for instance, the hard blue light of the desert Southwest falling in the Green Mountains, and the hallucinatory colors of Cape Cod, much loved by photographers, disappear when you go even a few miles inland. In Vermont the early-summer light is buttery and curiously curved, so that shadows have blunt and accommodating edges; you sometimes see this same rounded effect in Ireland, when the sun manages to come out at all. It may have something to do with rainfall. I don't know. Nobody talks about it much. Like the silence after the deep snow, it's just there, bringing with it an enveloping pleasure, as if light were woven, had weight, and could be folded like some precious textile.

Into this new medium we venture, looking for destinations. Summer, and especially the early part of summer, has a siren quality that drags everyone out on their annual field trips. One of the better ritual opportunities is Lilac Sunday at the Shelburne Museum where, if you have the dough for the admission, you can wander, sneezing, amid hundreds of different varieties of *Syringa*. If you can scare up a straw boater, ruffles, a long skirt, a parasol, or an ebony cane, so much the better, since dressing up is part of the Lilac Sunday gestalt. This annual costume drama doesn't really have much of a point—it's not a reenactment of anything other than a vague Victorian posturing—but it's fun to ooze across the lawn, nodding and chatting earnestly like a character on a work-release permit from a Henry James novel. Some people wouldn't miss it, any more than they would skip the fireworks on Independence Day.

I personally prefer a visit to the camera obscura. It's a perverse thing to do on that first sunny day, mostly because it invariably involves sitting in the dark, but this is my way of talking to the returning warmth and the lengthening day. Vermont's camera obscura is tiny, almost a toy, but we are lucky to have one at all—once fairly common, they have vanished from the landscape. When I talk about the one in Norwich, people look at me funny: Camera what? Does it take pictures? What are you talking about?

The camera obscura had its conceptual beginnings with Aristotle, who noticed, during a solar eclipse, that tiny images of the crescent sun were scattered across the ground under a tree. He was puzzled by the phenomenon and speculated it had something to do with the apertures created by the overlapping leaves, but he wasn't sure how, and he eventually left the problem where he found it and moved on to other things. But the observation was picked up again with a vengeance during the Renaissance—the properties of light were studied, lenses and mirrors were called in for assistance, and the resulting camera obscura became an important tool in the hands of people like Kepler, Leonardo da Vinci, Baptista Porta, and Vermeer.

The premise is simple: Light travels in a straight line. When the rays reflected from a bright object pass through a hole into a dark room, they don't scatter. Instead, they assemble on the opposite wall into an inverted color image of the thing itself, animated and a little grainy and upside down, and the result is a silent and washy portrait of the moving world, full of a watercolor light and eerily beautiful. The images move—soundlessly, as if without weight or consequence—and the simple fact that everything hangs downward from the ceiling adds to the oddness. This upside-downness can be a visual inconvenience, and when I visited a camera obscura in a senior center in Santa Monica, I saw it had been upgraded with a viewing table shaped like a shallow bowl—the viewer walks around the edges until the image is right-side up again. This camera also had a rotating turret so you could change the view by turning a crank. You could look out over the ocean, or the buildings on the boulevard, or watch the silent, endlessly turning Ferris wheel down on the promenade. The

Vermont camera obscura is a much more bare-bones example, but the effect, in the end, is the same: The simplest of all optical tricks imaginable becomes a kind of theft or at least an abduction. And while there are working camera obscuras in England, California, Wales, Hungary, Maine, and probably a few other places, none has the primitive, almost childish charm of this one. It sits on the shores of the Connecticut River in a merry little building that looks like a demented potting shed.

THE CAMERA OBSCURA EKES OUT a slender existence on the boundary between art and science—it's both the forerunner of the modern camera and the source of the subtle, haunting distortions of paintings like Vermeer's *The Girl with the Red Hat* and *View of Delft.* Portable camera obscuras were used widely by artists during the nineteenth century, and the artistic properties of the images, with their mix of suggestive blurriness and complete accuracy, made camera obscuras popular items with the public. They turned up in parks, at scenic overlooks, and at seaside resorts; the sign on one of these installations read, in part, "The most wonderful and enchanting exhibition. Marvelous miniature views of this lovely garden showing all of the people and children moving like fairies. Boats, foliage, flying birds, cattle, horses and carriages, waving flags, etc. Friends can be recognized, although so remarkably small as to appear extremely laughable." Admission was a dime, which in the late 1800s was not quite the chump change it is today.

People went to the camera obscura, in part, because it was a kind of precursor to television, and because it qualified as a curiosity, something all Victorians were inordinately fond of. But this business about spotting friends in the distance also points to another thing about the camera obscura that is not always obvious—it appealed to voyeurism. The camera obscura made it possible to see without being seen, and this secretive, once-removed quality certainly added another weird dimension to its charms. An 1890 cartoon from *Puck* magazine shows an amorous young man preparing to drape himself over a young lady. "Ah, Amelia," he sighs in the caption, "at last we are by ourselves, far from unsympathetic and prying eyes!" Yet there he is in the round bowl of the camera obscura viewer, the object of the scrutiny of enough people to start a baseball team. It's frankly unsettling, even if it is sort of funny, and it may tell us a little more about the dark side of the Victorian sensibility than we really need to know.

But like the small friends who appear extremely laughable, this seems like a trivial concern when in the presence of the thing itself. The camera obscura in Norwich is simple, almost primitive, when compared to the optically enhanced and mirrored specimens in swankier settings, but the end result is much the same: The magic lantern that is life throws its image on a darkened plane, and the longer you wait, the better it gets. It takes the eye a long time to really adjust to darkness, but once it has, the camera allows you to send your secondhand gaze east across the river or west toward the cheerful hulk of the Montshire Museum. The doors that control the tiny light holes open and close with amusing wooden *thunks*, as if some huge loom were in operation.

OUTSIDE SAN FRANCISCO A MINOR WAR is being waged over a camera obscura that is slated for demolition. As it has been slated before. The Giant Camera, which is shaped like a huge Kodak Brownie abandoned on its back, was once part of an amusement park called Playland. Playland went south in 1972 and was going to take the camera obscura with it, but a public campaign saved it and put it in the care of the Park Service. It sits on a high promontory overlooking Seal Rock on Point Lobos, and as architectural kitsch alone it almost certainly qualifies as a treasure. But the Park Service has its doubts, and wants to raze the building as part of the reno-vation of a nearby pile called the Cliff House—they seem to concede its cuteness but are strapped for money. Is it really worth maintaining? Still, at least part of its interest lies in the shortage of these devices, not just in the United States, but pretty much everywhere else as well. Jack and Beverly Wilgus, who travel all over the world to visit camera obscuras, report that the number of intact examples of the breed can be counted on the fingers of their four hands. If true, it is disturbing, and it makes me view the Norwich camera obscura with considerably more respect.

The debate over the cultural value of camera obscuras has certainly had its dismissive moments. During the 1972 discussion of the Giant Camera on Point Lobos, some letters to the editor talked about the camera's place in history and in the development of photography, others about the rare visual experience it offered. But just as many shrugged the whole thing off. If you want to look at the spectacular view, they seemed to be saying, why not step out into the sunlight and do exactly that? The dark room with its projected copy was only that—a copy. It teaches a lesson in optics, but the lesson is a simple one. What's the big deal?

The big deal, if there is one, may be embedded in the personal. The camera obscura offers marginal and obvious optics to our modern eyes and is pretty boring science if science is what you want. On one level, it's simply too easy to understand. But if it isn't science you come for, then the experience deepens: The complexity lies in what art historian

134

Sister Wendy Beckett calls the "silence of Vermeer." In her discussion of the riveting, selectively blurry realism of the Dutchman's paintings, she invokes another kind of world, both more mystical and, curiously, less fragile than this one. "He elides, of course, but we are unaware of it," she says in *The Story of Painting.* Vermeer's paintings have an authenticity and a visual authority that makes them utterly riveting, "and this sense of total truth," says Beckett, "offered to us through a reverence for what is bodily present, effortlessly acquires a sense of the spiritual."

I don't know about *effortlessly,* but it's not my place to argue with a nun. Still, Vermeer's artistic reputation and his reliance on the camera obscura to develop his paintings are two of art history's accepted facts; Marcel Proust named Vermeer's *View of Delft,* which was almost certainly done with the aid of the camera obscura, as the world's single greatest painting. We can concede that Proust was a strange writer, obsessed with digression, precision, analysis, and, most of all, memory. Yet we can also concede that, despite the chasm of time and intention between the two artists, both understood the linkage between image and afterimage, original and copy, that seems basic to the idea of artistic distance.

Of course, we should not necessarily revere the camera obscura because Vermeer used one, but we can still use the camera and ask ourselves what it is we see. On this sunny playground in Norwich, I see two children running, glad to be out in the spring air—they race inverted, with their heads downward, across an image washed in the browns and dull golds of a landscape on the edge of awakening. In their bright clothes they look like mobile Easter eggs, blurry and holographic. I can hear them yelling outside, but their second selves are silent, moving through a precise dreamscape in which their gestures of play seem fraught with intensity, packed with meaning. Inevitably, one of them yanks the door open, dissolving the image by adding too much light. She asks what I am doing here.

"Actually, I was watching you," I tell her. I explain briefly how the camera obscura works. "You can see it too. You have to wait, though, and let your eyes adjust to the dark."

"How long does that take?"

"Probably five minutes. About as long as two songs on the radio."

She shuts us in together and I am suddenly uncomfortable waiting in the dark with a complete stranger, however small and harmless she might be. It is uncomfortable for her, too—I may have looked like an acceptable grown-up at first, but now that she can't see me she can't really be sure. It's horribly awkward. In less than a minute she is out the door again, calling to her brother. "Hey guess what?" she tells him. "That lady in there, she's *spying* on us."

THE OTHER THING THAT HAPPENS on the brink of summer is that farms go out of business. In April and May it's perfectly possible to go to a herd or farm dispersal every day of the week. The notices in the newspapers are always compressed and precisely written: "140 head Holsteins, chain-tied, milked in parlor—will adapt to loose housing; 80 mature cows, nearly one half are first-calf heifers, farm raised with size, condition, and artificial breeding for years. 69 cows over 8000+ lbs. SCC 140,000–160,000; herd average 60 lbs. on round bale baleage. Herd split with good group fresh and also lots of fall cows. 15 big fancy heifers due August-September, also 26 big fancy open heifers, RTB; 20 heifers 3 to 6 months old. Sale by Ag Sales Unlimited, Newport, Vermont."

These notices are not meant to be demoralizing, but they are. Vermont's identity as an agricultural state, and—since the coming of the railroads—a dairy state, is under siege. There are a lot of reasons for this, and some of them are amazingly complicated, but the basic squeeze on farmers is that it now costs more to produce milk than that same milk fetches in the marketplace. For the small farmer the temptation is to produce more milk, even though this drives milk prices ever downward, and the trend has been for small farms to go under or be bought up by bigger farms, which at least have some competitive advantage in economies of scale. It's kind of a mess, and it's a mess that spills over onto other things like land-use legislation, economics, and tourism. Perhaps especially tourism, since it is the small family farm that has made the Vermont landscape what it is—a lovely, slightly drunken patchwork of woodlots, fields, crops, and grazing Holsteins, with a Greek Revival farmhouse as the aesthetic anchor.

There is a lot to understand about Vermont farming that isn't apparent from the interstate, or even from the mournful and sometimes angry opinion columns in the newspapers. Milk pricing structures favor the processors and handlers, and rising land values make it tempting to grow houses instead of silage or corn. But there is more. Jan Albers, in her clear and accurate history of Vermont's landscape, *Hands on the Land*, captures something essential about farming that emerged during the nineteenth century and still permeates how we think about farms today. "Landscapes begin in the human mind," she explains. "No age can claim to be fully conscious of its own actions, but some have the ability to think about what they are doing more than others." She points out that the prototypical Vermont farm was not an example of accidental beauty, but was a product of a new way of thinking about order, control, and planning. "As a product of its age," Albers says, "this kind of thought did not lend itself to an ecologically balanced landscape, but rather to a morally balanced one. A moral landscape was a rational, productive, and well-maintained landscape, with a proper mix of elements in an attractive form."

It is this moral dimension—this deep and largely unspoken conviction that Vermont ought to look and be a certain way—that gives farm and herd dispersal sales their emotional density. This is in spite of a surface festiveness on the day of the sale—there is a tent, often a striped tent, and a concession stand selling hot coffee and rubbery hamburgers with too much relish, and inside the tent there is a fenced platform, bedded with clean sawdust, that cows and heifers are decanted onto from the barn. They go up the ramp to the platform with varying degrees of reluctance and with the splayed, foursquare, scrambling gait that is the defining feature of a dairy cow. Once in this makeshift arena, they take in the crowd of bidders and bystanders with vaguely alarmed but mostly blank expressions. My foster mother had Ayrshires and loved them dearly, but to me all cows look the same except for obvious variations in breed and size, and I am always a little repelled by their nose-licking, their head-bumping, and their general lack of enterprise. But despite this, the sadness of the moment isn't lost on me, and I wonder what it is like for a cow to be wrenched from its familiar herd and dispersed.

We know, at least in the telling, what it is like for the farmers, since the media in Vermont is interested in capturing their feelings and opinions. Alan Brace, a Huntington farmer who sold off at the end of the 2003 mud season, told the *Burlington Free Press* that "There's ten reasons to stop, and there's one reason to stay. And that one reason is that I really love to do it." Brace, like most farmers, has had to work off the farm to keep it going. How many of us—except the artists we encountered in an earlier chapter—are willing to do this double labor? And the parallel may not end there, since losing a farm, for a farmer, may be exactly comparable to aphasia in writers or deafness in musicians. When the Martin farm in Rochester was sold off, the owner didn't even wait to count the auction money. He committed suicide instead.

The farm dispersal sale I attended recently definitely had its dispiriting aspects. The fine old barn was peeling, the fence lines drooped, and the pastures had jackstraw piles of lumber scattered here and there, as if these outbuildings and icehouses had simply imploded and were now working their way back into the soil. The stock trailers lining the road still looked serviceable and relatively new, but the bidding itself was careful and even a little listless; a lot of people seemed more interested in eating and talking. When the sun found a hole in the cloud bank, people came out of the tent and stood in it—it was intermittent, but when it came it was soft and bright, and the whole event took on a pensive rather than an acquisitive air. Two twentysomething herdsmen— one with neck tattoos and piercings like an overgrown mall rat—compare notes on their earnings, and by eavesdropping I learn that one makes $8.00 an hour, the other $8.50. "Which ain't bad," says the one. "Surely not," says the other. This exchange depresses me. Even with housing thrown in free, as it usually is, these do not strike me as incentive wages for the next generation of farmers.

Yet all is not sadness on this weekday morning, since mud season is over and the warmth of the day is spreading like a blanket over the yellow fields, and with it comes a kind of alertness, a generic brightening of spirits. Even the barn cats, which have been watching the auction from a careful distance, perk up a little: They have discovered how to get onto the top of the auction tent from a nearby shed roof. Four or five of them—barn cats are always difficult to count accurately—are using the striped, bouncy canvas as an impromptu trampoline. From below, their feet make dimples, as if some benign giant were poking the tent from above with a knitting needle, and, from outside the tent, it is possible to watch several cats in succession come to the edge and look down owlishly on the feed-capped heads of the assembled bidders. One pregnant tortoiseshell takes a careful patrol of the perimeter, balancing herself carefully, before she flops down, yawns, spreads her toes, and serenely falls asleep.

THE NEWS
FROM FROG CITY

IN 1884 THE VERMONT LEGISLATURE ran out of important things to do and turned its attention to the affairs of No Town. It was an inquiry that must have presented certain challenges, since there was no No Town on the map, no No Town on the tax rolls, and no No Town included in the charters of adjacent and legitimate places. But investigators were dispatched, and No Town was found, a forgotten rectangle of land that, for almost forty years, had been flying low and avoiding annexation or incorporation; No Town held a happy handful of Vermonters who seemed to percolate along very nicely in the absence of government. They raised their sheep, worked their sawmill, and minded their own business—it was, on the face of it, a small-scale Yankee utopia. This was especially true because, being off the map, they did not pay any taxes.

Now, this is the sort of thing that will always get legislators sitting up a little straighter in their chairs: *Look here,* said Montpelier, *this just won't do.* But when lawmakers decided that No Town should be annexed to Stockbridge, wails of protest rose from the residents; a Vermonter's preference for thinking outside the box extended to living outside it, too, especially if the outside of the box offered those particularly sunny vistas that do not include property taxes. The No Towners, determined to salvage something, stubbornly negotiated for five more years of tax abatement, and five years proved just long enough for the residents to finish their logging, eat their mutton, and quietly move away.

They may have moved on to Lost Nation, No Nothing, or Tommy Squatter; they may have vanished up the slopes of Delectable Mountain. Wherever they went, they took with them something essential, inventive, and inflationary. "Vermont," Esther Munroe Swift told me back in 1988, "has more place-names than anywhere else in the world."

"The world?" I asked.

"That's right," she said.

Esther Swift should know, since she is the author of *Vermont Place-Names: Footprints of History*, which is the final authority on the origins of names like Skunks Misery, Puddledock, and Billymead, and she likes to point out that the book, which has considerable heft, is not really complete. "When we started out, I collected the name of every bump, dent, and trickle," she said, "and we saw early on that it was getting out of hand. We had to develop rules about what could go in, what had to be deleted, just so you could fit it all in one volume." As it is, the book looks less like a book than it does like a doorstop. "And you can use it that way when you get bored with reading it," Swift said.

The odds of boredom are slender. Where else can you read about how Glover's Long Pond was transformed, early in the nineteenth century, to Runaway Pond? "On a fine June day in 1810, about sixty people started the ditching operation. All went well until the bottom of the channel they had dug suddenly seemed to dissolve: it was quicksand. Out rushed the whole lake, taking everything in its course, as a wall of water sometimes fifty feet high rushed to Lake Memphremagog. It took six hours for the water to dash the twenty-seven miles to the big lake, and there wasn't much left behind it in the valley—trees, stones and houses were all jumbled together." Runaway Pond, today, consists of the mess it left behind and a stone marker and sign—it doesn't actually have any water in it.

The Vermont passion for place-names is a product of Vermont geography: It's a place full of places. As Swift pointed out, "If you have a flat piece of empty land that's a couple of hundred or even a couple of thousand acres square, you can call it the Sahara and be done with it. But when you take that land and wad it up like a newspaper, then you have a chance to name every bump and crevice." It's an opportunity Vermonters have seized with both hands, and with a certain opinionated waywardness—if naming the animals was Adam's task, then naming all the places was almost certainly relegated to a Vermonter. Take, for instance, the Great Hardwick Post Office Muddle, another instance of what happens when government and the Vermont temperament collide.

It began innocently enough in 1810, when the Hardwick post office opened in East Hardwick, a village known locally as Stevensville. Samuel Stevens was a builder of mills and the town's most important citizen, and after a time the residents petitioned the postal authorities to change the name of the post office from Hardwick to Stevens.

For reasons best known to the postmaster general, the name was transformed to Stephens, a typographical error that infuriated the residents, who promptly petitioned to become Hardwick again. But in the meantime, in North Hardwick, a new post office had opened and it wanted to be called Hardwick. Since Stevensville had been vacillating between Hardwick and East Hardwick, perhaps Stevensville could let them use the name. Then the status of South Hardwick was brought into play—could this be Hardwick, too? A kind of potlatch ensued, with Hardwick bouncing from place to place until the locals eventually tired of it. When the dust settled, Stevensville was East Hardwick, North Hardwick was Hardwick, and South Hardwick was Lamoilleville.

Everything was peaceful until 1842, when the postal authorities intervened again. It was too confusing, they decreed, to have a Lamoilleville that was not in Lamoille County. (Chittenden, Vermont, is not in Chittenden County, but apparently they hadn't noticed yet.) Suddenly, Lamoilleville was South Hardwick, the delicate balance was upset, and the Hardwick shuttlecock was back in play. It's hard to be sure, but it does look like things intensified to the point where, from 1864 to 1867, there was no Hardwick at all, which probably sets a municipal record for keeping the ball in the air. Today the Hardwick post office is in Lamoilleville, and the East Hardwick post office is in Stevensville. North Hardwick, after retiring from the fray, seems to have vanished without a trace.

All this from a spelling error, but in simple error lies opportunity. Inside each Vermonter lies a No Towner—fractious and critical of bureaucracy. The No Town spirit was alive and well in Sudbury when a rocky, useless lump on the landscape was christened Government Hill. It's not good for much, but it's definitely there.

IN CORINTH, JUST WEST OF BRADFORD in Orange County, there is a village with the enchanting, nursery-rhyme name of Goose Green. Geese are bad-tempered—permanently insulted and full of false accusations—but it must be conceded that they look delightful from a distance on a grassy background. At first glance this seems to be what the name of this pretty hamlet is about. The truth, however, is more pragmatic and illuminating: One of the families in Goose Green did indeed raise geese, and when the geese were ready for market they had to be joined in huge flocks with neighboring geese and walked down the long, dusty road to Boston. As the flock progressed, its ranks grew, and just thinking about making a goose walk that far in the company of others gives me a headache, but that's not really the point. The point is that each owner used a marker to separate his geese from the others. The Corinth farmer eliminated any confusion about which geese were his by putting a streak of unambiguous green paint on one wing—and thus the name Goose Green.

In Vermont we call them as we see them; looking at the map, you get the feeling that the most common place name in Vermont is *mud*. There is Mud Pond, Mud Flat, Mud Hollow, Mud Island, and even Mud Point. *Mud* seems to be followed by *mill* (Mill River, Mill Village, Mill Brook) and *little*. There is Little Bluff, Little Panton, Little Equinox, and (of course) Little Mud Pond—I haven't come across Little Mud Mill Pond, but then I haven't been looking all that carefully. The ubiquity of *mud* and *mill* is probably self-explanatory, but what are we to make of Egypt,

Michigan, Chicago, and Rhode Island? These kinds of names are also abundant, and they refer to remote, vaguely exotic places that once took a certain fixity of purpose to get to. And often still do—one of the Michigans, high in the Green Mountains at the headwaters of the Tweed River, is now a collection of cellar holes; in the springtime a few lilacs still bloom, along with a single enduring daffodil, tucked up against a crumbling foundation. Farther up the road—if it qualifies as a road—were the hamlets of Philadelphia and New Boston. The intrepid explorer, armed with enough insect repellent, could conceivably visit the ruins of three great cities in a single day.

In these names are stories: Pumpkin Hill in Danville harks back to an eighteenth-century infestation of worms that ate everything in the fields except the pumpkins; this was followed by an influx of pigeons that ate the worms. The villagers lived on pumpkin and pigeon until the next harvest, which must have been boring but kept them alive. The town of Jamaica was not named ironically, although it certainly sounds that way; instead, *jamaica* is Natick for "beaver." The Lemon Fair River in Weybridge may have once been the Lamentable Affair River, which it sort of is, being rather sleepy and small, but it may also have been the *limon faire,* which means "to make mud" in French, proving that the state can mix water and dirt in two languages.

It sometimes seems that everyone—the Algonquin, the Iroquois, the French, and the English colonists—got a shot at Vermont place-names, and the colonists took extra swipes at the enterprise because, for a long time, there was a muddle over who Vermont actually belonged to. Grants in Vermont were made by New Hampshire, New York, and Massachusetts, and names like Bamf, Eugene, Kelso, Virgin Hall, Minto, and Socialborough all lie underneath the names that actually stuck, a toponymic palimpsest of human occupation. There's even a nonexistent place called Monro, which got talked about and thought about and written about in the editorial section of the newspaper, but never actually got fully spoken into being. Monro was the brainchild of four other towns—Bethel, Royalton, Randolph, and Tunbridge—and the idea was that each town would chip in a corner of itself and a new town would set up shop, thus making it much easier for the residents in the hinterlands to get to a village, conduct town business, and vote. This was a kind of No Towning in reverse, but it still apparently proved to be a challenge to the legislature, which, as we have seen, is not particularly light on its feet. Swift reports that the Monro campaign "was taken seriously and referred to committee; but the petition went around and around in the legislature and finally was dismissed in 1823."

PERHAPS ONE OF THE DANGERS of having so many place-names is that we may not notice when we are losing them. The town of Stowe once had inside its borders a Cape Cod, a Loomisville, a Nebraska, and a Moscow; now only Moscow remains. It seems perfectly plausible that place-names fade with the advent of velocity. If you drive through a town with six or seven villages, you do not necessarily experience them as individual places, but this is not the case when progressing more attentively on horseback or on foot. Of course, new names do spring up as we get more clustered and more urbanized, but too many of them seem to come from some prepackaged developer database that combines words and ideas in a kind of slack-jawed, Prozacky interchangeability: Bay Meadow, Meadowlark Run, Woodland Glen. If you put these place-names in a bottle and give them a good shake, all you get is more of the same: Meadowlark Bay, Woodland Run, and Meadow Glen. You can't tell them apart. Worse, you're not supposed to be able to.

Yet here I am on an early summer day in Frog City, a damp corner of Plymouth. When I made the turn off the main road, I naturally imagined soaring green towers and a bustling amphibian economy, but I'm not really disappointed—Frog City is pretty and peaceful, and I am quite sure the inhabitants are just lurking, waiting for the intruder to get bored and go away. Still, it's a good place to sit peacefully and unfold my map. The town of Plymouth, where Calvin Coolidge made his home, offers up any number of promising places: Tyson Furnace, Dublin, Ninevah, and a place called Tiny Mountain that actually looks pretty darn big. There's a Money Brook, which harks back to a band of counterfeiters, and there's a Plymouth Kingdom, where a gold mine used to be. I learn from reading Swift that the town was originally chartered as Saltash, and that the iron from the furnaces at Tyson were used to build the *Monitor*, that ungainly but effective war boat that was the Union's answer to the Confederate *Merrimack*—these two ironclads made maritime history when they faced off in 1862 in the Hampton Roads. Plymouth, at least for now, seems fairly safe from the Woodland Meadow Glen Run mumble, even if there is a big ski area in the next town over.

The persistence of place-names in Plymouth is not a trivial achievement—like the Michigan daffodil, there is something poignant about the small places of Vermont. They do not always coexist comfortably with trendy condos, and it sometimes seems that a new kind of No Towner roams the state, vaguely pleased with the scenery but not always completely clear where home is; the continuity of places depends on rootedness and a sense of ownership.

And, of course, on the postal authorities. "Did you know," Swift asked, "that if you tell people you live in Royalton, and then someone tries to send you something in the mail to Royalton, it may well come back stamped NO SUCH PLACE?" Yet Royalton is established, brick-built, and historic, the site of the 1780 Mohawk raid that took four lives and twenty-six prisoners, and was led—as these things sometimes were—by a British officer. Royalton even merits its own exit off the interstate, yet all the Royalton mail goes to South Royalton, which, perversely, is several miles due east.

It's hard to know whether to butt heads with the government or secede. "Let's close the borders," suggests Ernest Callenbach, author of *Ectopia,* who once referred to Vermont as Ectopia East. Maybe that, but maybe we could just reopen No Town. No Town, clearly, is a more sporting proposition.

Bullwinkle and the
Bucky Agenda

T HE NORTH COUNTRY MOOSE FESTIVAL, which is held each summer in the Northeast Kingdom and over the state line in northwestern New Hampshire, draws about 3,000 people. But no moose—this despite a moose-calling contest that is marked by a cascade of yodels, coos, and grunts. Moose, if the contestants are to be believed, sound a little like a cow that could use a laxative, and the contest triggers much applause and coaching from the bleachers. But all this calling gets no answer: No large beasts emerge from the surrounding woodlands, shambling on their long front legs and peering at the humans down their lumpy noses. Moose-calling prizes, it seems, are awarded on the basis of presentation, not results.

Moose, despite their comeback in recent decades, try hard to have as little truck as possible with humans. While it is true that they get hit on the interstate, mostly during mud season, this is mostly because they like salt and are attracted by the sodium content of the melting snow. This is why they can be seen poking around in the roadside culverts and slobbering intently on the guardrails, and they get hit because they are preoccupied, and because a Subaru doing 60 doesn't look to them like much to worry about. But this is mostly a seasonal aberration; the rest of the time they try to stay out of sight, living on scrub and wallowing in the wet places. When a moose wanders through town wearing a dazed expression, it may well have parasitic brainworm and not a powerful urge to socialize. A bull moose that made the news a few years ago by courting a Holstein on a farm in Shrewsbury was a confused specimen and perhaps even a debased anomaly—self-respecting moose have higher aspirations and better eyesight and would dismiss the celebrated cow, Jessica, as a complete skag. Moose offer an aloofness that approaches grandeur. We call, but the moose feels no obligation to answer. We drive, and the moose does not get out of the way.

This oblique majesty probably explains why the annual Moose Festival plays out the way it does, with its mix of success and failure. It certainly works hard to live up to its billing—the place is crawling with moosey memorabilia—but it's hard not to notice a Northeast Kingdom aftertaste of downscale camp to the proceedings. The Kingdom has its own hunting-camp aesthetic: Here you can purchase moose thermometers, moose throws, moose figurines, wooden moose with little clocks in their tummies, and all manner of craft items that are mostly about moose and sometimes about the north-woods culture that has sprung up around them. In one display booth the duck decoys snuggle among the heavy-duty scrapers that will squeegee the mud off your boots; in the next a tinny little biplane made of empty beer cans catches the breeze in its propeller—it's proof, if we need it, that you can recycle something you don't want into something else you don't want if you just have the right tools handy. Under a large tent are samples of mock-moose stew prepared by area restaurants; when asked what goes into mock-moose stew, the chefs offer a little shrug. Not moose—real-moose stew is, of course, both out of season and possibly sacred. Two turns around the grounds turn up only one actual moose, a stuffed calf, that is part of a display of taxidermy. It draws a modest crowd that stands in a reverent semicircle, as if waiting for its health to improve.

If you want to see an actual, living moose, then you have to go looking for one, and the festival moose tours carry the uninitiated to the buggy shores of Great Averill Pond near Canaan, Vermont, and to "Moose Alley" near the Connecticut Lakes in New Hampshire. There you can perhaps see the moose chowing down on the shrubbery—the word *moose* derives from an Algonquian word for "eater of twigs," and a grown twig eater packs in forty to sixty pounds of roughage a day. But be warned: These junkets are not for the wuzzyheaded. Most of the tours depart at 6:00 A.M., which is apparently when the moose are leaving for work; there is also a 4:00 P.M. moose tour that presumably catches the moose on the way home.

YET THE MOOSE FESTIVAL, DESPITE ITS NAME and its abundance of moose iconography, is not really much about moose at all. The moose, it seems, is mostly a rallying point, an easy excuse to get together, pitch some tents, play a little music, and eat fried dough. Festivalgoers may wear brown fuzzy feed caps with floppy antlers, but they spend the bulk of their time enjoying the sunshine and wandering with a kind of aimless serenity down rows of gleaming antique cars. These cars, lovingly restored, are one of the real cornerstones for the festival—over the course of this three-day event, these cars will have cruised, paraded, stood at attention, and gone to Our Lady of Grace Shrine for the Blessing of the Autos. A "Christmoose" crafts fair is framed by an all-you-can eat breakfast, a rubber ducky race, hot-air balloon rides, a street fair, and a chance to take a horse-and-buggy ride. By the time you get to the '50s costume contest—to the poodle skirts, hair gel, and pointy shoes—the connection to the mighty moose is largely rhetorical.

This may be why the main Saturday event, held at the Murphy Dam just over the Vermont state line in Pittsburg,

New Hampshire, does not feel like a gathering of red-suspendered, flash-orange sportsmen so much as a congregation of vague affiliates, perhaps a class reunion or a company picnic. There is meeting and greeting; children move in packs and stain their lips with blue cotton candy; a spirited game of *bocce* erupts without warning and ticks away the summer afternoon. With a small flourish and a lot of squeak, Bobo the Clown makes balloon animals that are said to be giraffes and ostriches, but all look about the same and fit nicely on a child's head like a deranged tiara. There is a dunking booth with a jeering teenager whose job it is to insult people into buying three softball throws for a dollar; there is an endless loop of old Beach Boys tunes wafting from the loudspeakers. There is bright sun. There are boiled franks. There is a long line for a taste of free ice cream. On the surface the Moose Festival proceeds with the relentless predictability of a second-tier county fair. *Why are we here?*, we ask ourselves as we chew and tromp a little dutifully among the booths. *What's here that isn't everywhere?*

Yet the Moose Festival does offer its own kind of pleasure. Where else, for instance, can you see a hotly contested event in backing up an automobile? If you think this sounds a little wonky, then you're right, it is, and it works like this: An orange basketball is placed on a pole, and a competitor proceeds in reverse to the starting line. There the rear-view mirror is draped in an ominous black cloth and a signal is given. The idea is simple: Back the car as close as possible to the pole without knocking off the ball. Yet this very simplicity brings with it a kind of stately complication, and after each attempt the results are measured, written carefully on clipboards, and announced over a loudspeaker. There are daredevils who back up quickly and stop with a dramatic little crunch as the tires lock against the gravel; there are wild-guessers who proceed on raw intuition; there are steady executive types who bring a copilot who, through some quirk in the rules, is allowed to simply turn around and look out the back window and tell the driver what to do. This certainly shows that you can make a game out of anything; the great Vermont genius, as we have seen, is to make much out of little. The competition draws a large crowd, a lot of running commentary, boos, and cheers.

As fun goes, this may be a little on the slender side for certain palates, but it may be useful to remember that we are now in a part of the world that has peculiar tendencies. For one thing, this is the corner of Vermont that has more boundaries than it probably knows what to do with— Canaan, in the far northeastern corner of Vermont, protrudes like a hitchhiker's thumb into New Hampshire; less than a mile away, its northern border snuggles up to Canada. The area is also host to the forty-fifth parallel, which places it exactly halfway between the North Pole and the equator.

All these delineations bring not certainty but a kind of blurriness. Since you can't go far in any direction without crossing some sort of line, the lines seem to be both everywhere and curiously meaningless, so that Moose Festival parades sometimes begin in one state and end in the other. And boundaries are changeable and subject to opinion: In 1829 some of the folks in the area seceded and declared themselves the United Inhabitants of the Indian Stream Territory. Then, eleven years later, they decided they weren't, or they forgot about it, or it was just one more thing to keep track of, and the normal muddle reasserted itself. Knowing where you are, and perhaps where to stop, may have a certain resonance here that is not found elsewhere. If they want to practice backing up their cars with infinite accuracy, more power to them.

This minimalism seems to thrive in the maximum environment of the Kingdom, a place where people are thin on the ground and the trees are thick. This is logging country, getting-by country, the country of long distances between small villages. A recent Fodor's guide to Vermont goes on at some length about the region's poverty but somehow fails to notice its over-the-top independence, its intransigence, its tangled beauty. And its absolute practicality—as the day heats up, it's hard not to notice that there are more kids lining up to be dunked than there are people paying for a chance to

administer a dunking. If you're hot and you just want to cool off, who cares how it happens?

IF YOU COME FROM SOME BUSIER, DENSER PLACE, the Vermont countryside can sometimes look like the Empty Quarter—there's a sparseness that can be unnerving, and it's not unusual to have to drive forty miles for coffee filters. It particularly seems to get on the nerves of visitors from out of state. "Why," someone from downcountry once asked me, "isn't someone *doing* something with all these fields and everything?" I looked around at all these fields and everything and it seemed to me like lots was being done with them—they were supporting woodlots and growing hay and pushing up corn and vegetables—but when I go to the Kingdom I remember this comment and think I understand what it means. There's a certain comfortable density that meets the eye in a pleasing way; too much stuff brings on a feeling of claustrophobia and impatience, while not enough stuff makes us uneasy, hungry for signs of human occupation. Just as southern and central Vermont look pretty skimpy to a visitor from New Haven, Connecticut, the Kingdom looks sparse to a Vermonter from Washington County, a place outfitted with at least one shopping mall and a small but ongoing traffic snarl that goes by the name of Montpelier.

This lack of density makes it easy to underestimate the durability and depth of the Kingdom, ticking along at its own pace and with its own economy. The Kingdom is almost a theme park of scarcity—it's about working three jobs and keeping chickens and somehow getting by. Casual and a little grubby, the Kingdom is a natural magnet for people who prefer undecorated lives, but it is also full of wily, intense passions, and it's probably no accident that I was in a diner in St. Johnsbury when I first heard the story of the white mule, which goes, more or less, like this:

It seems that Bucky had gone over the hill on business and, coming home, he spied a white mule out at pasture and simply fell in love. It was a big mule, white as snow, with as close to the look of eagles as a mule can muster. So Bucky went to the farmhouse and offered the mule's owner $150, cash, right then, to buy it, saying he'd come on back in three days with the trailer. On his return, the farmer had some bad news—in the interim, the white mule had colicked and died. The farmer had thought to bury it but eventually decided not to: "I figured," he explained to Bucky, "that since you already paid me for it, it was your mule that was dead, not mine."

Bucky was glum because he loved that mule, but he thought for a while and decided that he had the trailer ready and would take it home anyway. So they scooped up the beautiful white mule with the bucket loader and put it inside. And the next day

Bucky was all over town with his posters: WIN A WHITE MULE, $1.00 A CHANCE! DRAWING ON WEDNESDAY. Bucky sold a lot of tickets—who wouldn't want a pure white mule?—and about a week later at the ham supper he ran into the farmer who sold it to him. "I see you had yourself a raffle," the farmer said.

"That's right," Bucky replied. "I sold just about 200 tickets."

"Then there must have been just about 200 people kind of upset about getting a dead mule," said the farmer.

"No," said Bucky. "Only one."

"So what did you do?" asked the farmer.

"The only thing I could do," Bucky said. "The honest Vermont thing was to give him his dollar back."

This sly little story, with its aftertaste of vinegar, is about the twining together of passion and commerce—it's Bucky in love, and Bucky making good on his investment—and something about its hardness and sweetness seem to me to perfectly mimic the balance of life in the Kingdom. Tom Weakley, the Vermont storyteller who includes the white mule in his repertoire, once commented on public radio that stories like this one are widespread and very old: "They just travel around the country and around the world. This is the Vermont version." I was sorry to hear that; I wanted the story not only to be local, but true.

But the Bucky agenda is alive and well and seems to be

operating in a recent newspaper item about Terry Prue, a man who runs a glass-repair operation in Newport. There is a picture of Prue in the *Barton Chronicle*, smiling broadly and proudly holding an implement that looks like a doubtful union between a clarinet and a hedge trimmer, gussied up with mysterious nozzles and dials. The photo caption says that Prue "picked up [the object] at a yard sale a few years ago for 25 cents. Ever since then he has been trying to figure out what it is. He hasn't had any luck. Many people have taken guesses, Mr. Prue said, but he hasn't found anybody who has been able to give him a firm answer. Some people think it's some type of homemade musical instrument, while others have speculated that it might be a farm implement such as some type of sprayer. If anybody has any idea what it is or would like to study it closer, the object can be seen at his business, Glass Medics, on Derby Road." Some of the happiness radiating from Prue is the natural joy of a businessman who got his company name in the paper without paying a dime, but only some—the rest really is grounded in the object itself, which is strange and wonderful. Whatever it is, it is definitely worth a lot more than a quarter. He holds it reverently; it is the white mule of yard-sale curiosities.

The hard work of living in the Northeast Kingdom obviously has its own satisfactions, sufficient for the people who live there. As the Moose Festival winds down, it takes on a drowsy, underwater quality—sleepy children really do fall asleep, without weepy preliminaries, in the shade of the pines next to the sluiceway. Others make the short climb to the top of Murphy Dam, and from this high perch you can see the expanse of Lake Francis, its shores completely free of clutter: no docks, no floats, no cottages. And no moose, either. It sometimes seems that the object of the three days of festival is just another assemblage, or perhaps another white mule. Like much of the Kingdom—and like much of the Moose Festival—it may be easy to dismiss this vista as undercooked, perhaps even uninteresting, but the folks who go up there stay a long time, looking at nothing, and seem perfectly satisfied. As an aesthetic it's mildly contagious: Bobo the Clown makes his final balloon animal, which is said to be a swan and is indistinguishable from the giraffes and ostriches, while clumps of contented but pragmatic people find their slow way back toward their cars. "A good one," they tell each other, nodding. "A lot like last year." The old cars fire up their engines and begin a stately, throbbing exodus, and turning left and right out of the gates they pass one of the Kingdom's ubiquitous orange-diamond signs: MOOSE CROSSING, it says. NEXT 8 MILES.

The Care and Feeding
of John Deere

THE RULE WHILE I WAS GROWING UP was that the tractor lived indoors and the cars sat in the driveway, exposed to the weather. My foster father explained this housing arrangement by pointing out that the tractor had to start reliably in all weather, all the time—driveways must be plowed, brush hauled, pastures mowed, and trees dragged to the woodshed for slaughter—while cars were the lightweights, for frolics and errands. They were decorative, expendable, even luxurious, with their heaters and radios and conveniences. Cars would not go anywhere without the tractor, especially if the snow lay deep on our long, hilly driveway.

The tractor that lived in this relative lap of luxury was a 1957 Ford Powermaster 821 with all manner of attachments, sort of like a vacuum cleaner. I was not permitted to drive it and didn't want to—it was hungry looking, with its see-through engine and narrow nose like a greyhound, plus I knew my father worried every time somebody besides him fooled with the tractor. It made a lot of noise but had a delicate constitution; it also had the original gray paint, in good condition and with handsome red detailing, which he took a secret pride in. The tractor reposed in the stable, surrounded by its implements, and it even got a bath every now and again.

I didn't know it then, but my father was exhibiting mild but undeniable symptoms of tractor illness, which can tiptoe up behind you and gradually take over, much like a growing interest in all the two-letter weirdo words you can use while playing Scrabble. Still, I never questioned the wisdom of tractor pampering until I was in my forties, when I met someone who took me (and my old Subaru) to an actual car wash, where we water-cannoned off at least four layers of indeterminate gray stuff and discovered a great deal of rust underneath, not an entirely fun revelation. This same person also advanced the strange idea that cars ought to live indoors, and he said that this was what garages were for. This struck me as interesting if a little far-fetched—I'd seen garages at my friends' houses, but had an idea they were for storing skis and freezers.

But tractor illness did come to me, briefly, on the summer afternoon of the antique tractor pull. It could be that you only really catch it when you gather a lot of very distinctive tractors in one place. Antique machines—this is defined as any machine from before 1960—have a certain patina, an honorable sheen of use, that reminds me of oiled leather, and there's something genuinely thrilling about their size and their individuality. A joyous fever sets in as the monsters start to growl and crawl and rumble across the competition field; when you stand among them, the ground vibrates with their purring. Each engine really sounds different. Some of them say *tuck-tuck-tuck,* and some of them say *bum-bum-bum,* and some of them say flatulent, complex things that probably can't be transcribed without offending someone. Their human attendants stand and admire, their fingers tucked, farmer style, into their back pockets, talking earnestly but inaudibly. Their voices are dwarfed by the benevolent metal beasts that raise their voices in a chorus to the sky.

AGRICULTURE BRINGS WITH IT a certain aesthetic, but many of our prettified and romantic ideas about agriculture are pure piffle. The yeoman farmer with his dog, his hoe, and his straw hat is derived mostly from preindustrial paintings; modern farmers are businessmen in feed caps and steel-toed boots messing around with loud, practical machinery. This is why when Warren Preston, a Randolph Center farmer and one of the founding lights of the Vermont Agricultural Museum, talks about "Keeping a living history, keeping the connections to farming alive," he is referring to a connection without much quaintness. The fledgling museum, which sponsors the antique tractor pull, aspires to be a collection of heavy, ham-fisted, and practical equipment—sprayers, balers, cultivators, and manure spreaders—that may someday serve as a kind of counternarrative to places like the Billings Farm and Museum in Woodstock, where nineteenth-century tools and costumes are so lovingly displayed. It's not that the Billings Museum efforts are wrong—they go to some trouble to see that they are historically correct—but they are prettified. Preston's ideas about the Vermont Agricultural Museum are not. This museum will be harder and more muscular and about hum-ming beasts that leave a deeper imprint on the land.

The museum was incorporated in 1993 as a charitable and educational nonprofit with a mission to collect and dis-play farming artifacts and to provide educational materials. Now, seven years later, the museum, as a practical matter, does not exist. "We finally bought the land in the summer of 1999," says Preston, "and the town of Randolph helped out with the financing, but we are still amending and working on the planning and the land-use permits. This part has been an education for us. It's been complicated." Equally daunting are the financial logistics—Preston estimates the museum board needs to raise about $800,000 to build the museum structure and make the needed site improvements. The goal is to develop the fifty-one-acre site in Randolph Center so that there are demonstration fields, displays, a gift shop, and parking. "Almost everyone we have talked to has been supportive," says Preston. "By this I mean Rural Development, the town, the Department of Agriculture, the chamber of commerce, Soil Conservation, banks, and businesses. We seem to have everything we need except the money." He frowns when he says *money*. The word worries him.

The museum's annual tractor pull is about money, but not very much of it—for three bucks you get two days of unrelenting growling. It's a spectacle that includes tests of driving skill, tractor games, garden tractors, tractors by weight, tractors by age, and tractors standing in rows for our general edification. The setting for the 2000 pull is at the top of the world, in a large green field with long views to the south and west to Pico and Killington. Tents have been raised, and flags, so that the event has a heraldic air, like a jousting contest. The long pulling pit with its orange cones looks curiously dangerous, and the weight sled the tractors will hitch to has a name: "The Little Humiliator." It's a kind of tractor rodeo, and as the games begin it becomes an essay in the variety, poise, and expressiveness of individual pieces of machinery. Most of the tractors are battered, patched and scarred with honest labor and seem curiously alive even when they are not actually running.

One specimen, a carefully restored 1938 John Deere A, takes the top pulling prizes in two categories, dragging the sled steadily and earnestly across the field; the machine is owned by Gene Vossler of Morrisville and is the oldest tractor in the competition. The Deere says *rum-rum-rum*; the next tractor to pull, a 1958 Oliver, says *able-bodied, able-bodied, able-bodied*. When it reaches the far limit of its pulling abilities, the Oliver lifts its front wheels about a foot off the ground. I know it's a machine, but for a moment it looks like a pony. I want one, almost desperately, and when I say this out loud, a young and lively farmer offers to show me a tractor he has back on the home farm. He's ready to part with it if I'm interested. I don't want to explain to him that I live in town on a quarter-acre lot. Instead, I want to see the tractor.

WARREN PRESTON ALSO HAS THE ILLNESS, but his symptoms are under firm control. "The idea," he says, "is to collect the oral history of farming and make these videos, and show them so that people see the connection between the machines and a whole way of life. We have more than just tractors being donated—we have balers and choppers and all kinds of tools—and we want to be able to show the videos and pictures and have visitors understand that internal-combustion machinery is what made Vermont agriculture what it is."

When we think about what Vermont agriculture is, we mainly think about Vermont agriculture being in some kind of trouble. There is trouble with debt, trouble with growth, and trouble with the nonrelationship between prices and the cost of production. There is even trouble with hiring skilled help and coping with neighbors—agriculture is noisy and fragrant, and in the twenty-first century it's hard to sell people on a profession that does not offer full dental and paid vacations. Preston doesn't talk about these things, but they are implicit. When farms die, something critical dies with them, since farms grow not just food but also social stability. They are the tough, stringy fiber that binds together rural communities, especially in New England where most farms are still small and family-owned. And as Preston's battered hands and face remind me, one of the many crises in farming is about death, since the average age of a farmer in the Northeast is fifty-five, and only 8 percent of all farmers are under thirty-five, a drop of almost 50 percent in the past decade. This is problematic, since there is no next generation on the farm, and people who used to be accountants and auto-repair specialists find it hard to come in from the outside and see if farming suits them. Rising land values and drooping farm infrastructure—things like credit, equipment, and technical support—make it hard to start a farm; in 1970 you could buy Vermont farmland for $224 an acre, while in 2000 you had to fork over $1,640 for the same parcel. It seems that everywhere you poke at farming, a little more of the stuffing comes out, and these bad conditions sometimes mask the reality that there were times when things were worse, and that the advent of heavy machinery made farming both easier and more profitable. The Vermont Agricultural Museum's emphasis on postwar agriculture, with its industrial overtones, is without nostalgia but historically sound.

I ask Preston if the museum's permitting problems and money woes discourage him and he says, frankly, that they do. "I won't say it hasn't been difficult. It has. But we just have to keep working on it and working on it." *Working on it* is a farmer's mantra—like running his dairy farm, it's repetitive, stressful, and a test of tenacity, but as sometimes happens it does seem to have its interesting philosophical moments. The museum recently applied to became a member of the local chamber of commerce, despite the obvious absence of any ticket sales, any exhibit space, or any programming. The chamber played along, probably working on the theory that an idea like this one, vigorously manipulated, can acquire its own weird reality. It certainly seems real enough when the antique tractors begin thrumming, calling, and milling around on the bluish, lumpy grass.

A QUICK NOSE COUNT OF SPECTATORS makes it clear that, even with entry fees from the drivers, the antique tractor pull is better than a bake sale but nowhere near as good as a benefit concert or a high-stakes raffle. Vermont is not really a poor state—or at least not dirt poor—but it is a place where discretionary money is thin on the ground. People generally earn less and pay more—it costs a lot of money to stay warm in the winter. There was a humorous song going around during the last recession with a refrain to the effect that we live in a Third World country and we just don't know it. It struck a little bit of a nerve, but it also reinforced that living here is a *choice*. While it's true that every single one of us could move to Boston and make a lot more dough, we all know that we'd then have to live in Boston. But these same spectators, who probably would have been willing to pay five bucks a head, are happy where they are. It's a good day, as soft as butter and with clouds stacking up over the mountains to the southwest; from this high meadow you can see the brick-and-steel, postmodern campus of one of the state colleges, the rows of granite stones in the Vermont Veterans Cemetery, and the sun flashing off any number of silos. My partner, who seems to be as content with the proceedings as I am, recognizes a winning driver in one of the late heats. "That guy was the seller's lawyer when I bought my house," he says, a little surprised. "I didn't know he had a farm." Of course it's possible he doesn't—that he sold the heifers years ago but held on to the tractor because his illness would not permit him to let it go.

The end of the first day of the Vermont Agricultural Museum Field Days is disrupted by an accident—Francis King of Milton is badly injured while loading his tractor onto a flatbed trailer that was parked on a hill. The front wheels lifted as he guided his machine up the ramp; this same lift, which seemed so animate and charming while the pull was in progress, turned into menace as the rig overbalanced and flipped backward. King was trapped beneath his tractor for about fifteen minutes while the other drivers worked frantically to get him free. An ambulance took King away, and the crowd, shaken, sadly dispersed. They would talk about Francis King on the way home in the pickup, and compare his accident to other accidents. This, too, is a part of farming, but I read in the paper that the crowd came back again in force on Sunday.

THE LONG FAREWELL

BECAUSE VERMONT SUMMERS ARE SHORT, the smell of autumn can be caught around the edges of the breeze by Labor Day. This scent—a mix of hay bales, ammonia, and coffee grounds—arrives obliquely but unmistakably after the first cold rain, and within a week a few trees, usually the stressed ones, will display a flash of yellow fingernails. Autumn has become Vermont's defining season. It's the time of year most often seen on calendars, and it's reached the point where, when you say the name of the state, the main thing that probably comes to the public mind is a perfect orange pumpkin on a granite doorstep artfully surrounded by red and gold maple leaves. These stone steps often lead upward to a wide porch with a swing and two Adirondack chairs, one with a novel facedown on the arm next to a streaming mug of tea. Not to criticize—these things almost certainly exist somewhere—but the evocative, idealized content of this image leaves too little to the imagination. Autumn, for me and many other people, is the time to hit the Kmart and invest in an expensive, high-powered squirt gun.

My problem is a common one: As the growing season explodes into final ripeness, the full garden brings Bambi down from the woodlands just beyond the back fence. I live in the state capital, and we are not supposed to shoot off live ammunition in residential neighborhoods, but Bambi is doing really terrible things to my perennials, and Bambi's mother is looking on in serene approval, flicking her flat tail. I've had it up to here with the both of them, and after some careful comparison-shopping I pick out a high-end rifle with a small battery-powered faux-laser beam; at dusk, when Bambi is hungriest, I can flick this on and put a red dot right between Bambi's beautiful round eyes. When it's pumped up to maximum pressure, this gun will shoot a narrow and powerful stream of water about fifty feet, and the effect on Bambi can be spectacular. Deer are elegant movers, with a wonderful, springy way of going, but in the waning days of August the squirt gun triggers a raw and scrambling adolescent panic that is gangling and disorganized and very gratifying. I am sorry to report that by the first frost this effect has worn off—I can still move Bambi along with my water gun, but he is no longer horrified. He keeps right on chewing as he exits the yard, and he looks back at me over his shoulder resentfully. Something in the set of his neck tells me he will be back after some seemly interval. This explains why the gun lives on the back porch, always loaded and ready for action, but I'm not sure anything can explain my thrilled obsession with protecting my shaggy stand of plants. Maybe this isn't about greenery so much as it is about territory and the adrenaline of the hunt. I put a canvas shoulder strap on the gun—cannibalized from a dead piece of luggage—and hold the weapon close to my body as if it were an AK-47. Head down and eyes wide open, I stalk Bambi from behind a hedge of scarlet burning bush while my partner, weak with laughter, watches from the house. I have no time and no inclination for porch swings and mugs of tea.

But I'm not a complete brute, and the quiet and smoky farewell of autumn isn't completely lost on me. Fall, which seems to run a minimum of ten weeks here, is not only longer than summer but more poignant as well. It's the time of year to store up acorns, pause in graveyards, and play cello suites in the evenings. The foliage—called, with a grunt of respect, "the color"—can be rich and dizzying in a good year, with a vividness that makes you think there might be something wrong with your eyes. It vibrates along the optic nerve and shimmers with a kind of controlled hysteria, a red and gold shrieking in the trees. Despite the obvious thrill, it's almost a relief when it begins to settle down to a more conversational umber.

ONE OF THE AUTUMN GRAVEYARDS I like to pause in is in Middlebury, to make a visit to the mummy's grave. How it got there is something of a long story. It all began in December 1886, when a fellow named Henry Sheldon got a chance to buy an Egyptian mummy for $20. It wasn't a bad price, so he jumped at it—Henry Sheldon was exactly that sort of man. He'd been collecting stuff for years, and going about it with a kind of unhinged gaiety. His goal in life, it seemed, was to fill up his house and his life with *things*—with letters, spoons, tools, flyers, books, furniture, clothes, toys, games, coins, shoes, and pretty much anything else that crossed his path. Documents about Vermont were a specific passion, and particularly the paper ephemera—programs, almanacs, and town reports—that might otherwise have ended up in the dump or the incinerator. He knew, back at the turn of the century, what most of us would not learn until much later, that history is often to be found in papers that, at first glance, look like the perfect thing for the bottom of a birdcage.

Because Sheldon had spent a good part of his life gathering up any cultural artifact he could get his hands on, he probably qualifies as at least slightly off the beam. Stories are told of him, aging and growing deaf, waylaying the good people of Addison County as they cleaned their attics and put their school budgets in the woodstove. And even though his first focus was on Vermontiana, he also wanted, it seemed, at least one of everything else, and this apparently included wanting a mummy. If you have an acquisitive spirit, it seems a perfectly natural thing. Sheldon Museum librarian Polly Darnell writes, in "The Founding of the Sheldon Museum," that his interest in local objects spread outward to the things he felt that every museum really ought to have. This included "mummies, Indian artifacts, and an invitation to the trial of Guiteau," the man accused of assassinating President Garfield. He had "so many objects out of wood from William Alden's house that one gets tired of running across them," she says, but with what seems like affection, not exasperation. After 1882 he put it all in a roomy brick house in downtown Middlebury—the future Sheldon Museum—but the $20 mummy, along with a lot of other miscellaneous stuff, ended up in the attic.

Mummies are weird. We think of them as taking the lead in a certain sort of horror picture where they come back to life, wave their bandages, and exact revenge. Even well-behaved mummies like King Tut come with obscure curses and sinister eyebrows; they straddle, like the season, the blurry line between life and death. This may be why we hardly ever think of mummies as being small children, but that is what Sheldon's mummy was—a two-year-old that had been sadly damaged by time and transit. This damage lowered the eventual purchase price, according to Sheldon's letters, to $10. Shortly after it arrived, Sheldon wrapped his "little girl baby 3500 years old" in wire screen, apparently to hold her together. This is a frankly pathetic detail—human remains in chicken wire—and the child was probably only briefly displayed in the museum before being sent upstairs. There it stayed, mostly forgotten about, until 1945.

This was when George Mead, the president of the Sheldon Museum's board of trustees, reported to the board that the mummy "was in a sorry state of disrepair." The Vermont climate had done what the Vermont climate seems to do to everything. Fluctuating temperature and humidity in the attic had caused the embalming resins to run and pool on the wooden board the child lay on. Mead and the curator, Florence Allen, without going into too many disgraceful details, indicated to the trustees that the body was losing its integrity and that "the time had come when we must dispose of the Egyptian mummy."

How *do* you dispose of a mummy? It's a question with a lot of possible answers, and, as with most things, it depends on who you are. Mead was apparently a thoughtful and meticulous man. First, he had the writing on the board the child rested on translated, and this writing indicated that this was the body not of a girl, as Sheldon had thought, but of a "young prince," and more specifically the son of Sen Woset III, who ruled Egypt in the Twelfth Dynasty. The child's name was Amun-Her-Kepesh-ef; he had been taken from the family tomb in Dashur in the mid-1800s by grave robbers and had moved through the antiquities pipeline to Paris and then, eventually, to New York. By the time the archaeologist Jacques de Morgan formally excavated the tomb of Sen Woset in 1894 and declared it empty, the prince had already been in Sheldon's collection for nearly a decade. Thus we are reminded, again, of how the profit motive moves faster than your average archaeologist. But Mead, while investigating the background of the mummy he now needed to dispose of, never lost sight of the plain fact that the mummy was once a small human being. Again: How, exactly, do you dispose of a mummy?

One of the likable things about Vermont is that you can do what Mead did next and not get into six kinds of trouble over death certificates signed by attending physicians. Because he did what he clearly believed was the correct, humane, and theologically defensible thing—he arranged to have the child cremated, and then he buried the ashes in his own family plot in the Middlebury cemetery. This was generous—plots cost money and cremation does, too—but you can tell, from an interview he gave to the *Ford Times* in 1950, that this gesture had nothing showy or theatrical in it. He did this because it was the proper and loving thing to do. He talks, in this interview, about how he made a hole and put the scanty, charred creature into it, and how some of the child's ashes were carried away on the wind as he buried them. He said that this was a part of cremation, and a good part. The rest he mixed into the earth with his hand before covering the boy over, and he clearly enjoyed, in a melancholy and moral way, the task he had set for himself. He had paid due respect to someone small, fragile, and a long way from home.

THE MIDDLEBURY MUMMY IS MORE than a curiosity, although it is a curiosity and lots of people visit the grave. The stone Mead erected for the child is modest but genuinely interesting: Here in a Christian cemetery in Yankeeland we find carvings of the *ba*, the bird of the soul, and the *ankh*, the Egyptian symbol for life. The text on the stone offers names we are not sure how to say out loud—Amun-Her-Khepesh-ef himself, Sen Woset III, his father, and Hator Hotpe, his mom—and with a date that looks all right until we look at it again, carefully. It's not 1883, but 1883 B.C.—the occupant of this grave is 4,000 years old. To add to the pleasure, Amun-Her-Kepesh-ef appears to have, as a neighbor, a veteran of the Spanish-American War. On the oddity scale, it's up there.

Oddities, to some degree, are what collecting is all about, although Henry Sheldon was himself a strange duck, even among collectors. We think of collecting as being the lifework of the very rich, yet Sheldon started out on the poorer end of the spectrum; he was not an Electra Havemeyer Webb, perhaps Vermont's most famous wealthy magpie and the founder of the Shelburne Museum. He did have pockets, but they were not deep. Over the course of his life, Sheldon worked on the home farm and for the postal service, speculated in sawmills and real estate, ran a bookstore, sold musical instruments, and lost a staggering sum of money on a marble quarry in Shoreham. He once lost a job because of a youthful, irresistible compulsion to go to Albany to collect autographs, and because he had to build an organ, apparently without delay. Another employer despaired of "the time Henry spends in reading" and of his "too many outside interests." Don't we all know someone like this, fraught with energetic distractibility? Most of us do—they turn into people who own 4,000 salt-and-pepper shakers and cartons of Confederate scrip and license plates from every state in the Union.

Yet Sheldon was different. He seemed to feel—and somehow conveyed to his future trustees—that the real life of objects depended on the lives of the people who had handled them, and that remarkable things were often masquerading as something quite ordinary. And, perversely, that the opposite was equally true: Even such a remarkable object as an Egyptian mummy was a child first, and royalty later. This attitude is infused into every room of the Sheldon

Museum, where there is a plainspoken and trusting quality to many of the things on display, and this quality is reinforced in the Sheldon archives, where a passion for having things is clearly secondary to the passion for declaring their identity, naming their past, their owners, and their use.

As for the mummy, the file on it tells us that the boy's name is derived from the Egyptian god Amen, who was the hidden god and the god of winds. The child in the attic, it seems, "was his strong right arm"; to be completely thorough, we are also offered a translation of an Egyptian hymn to Amen: "I call upon thee," it says, "when I am in distress . . . that thou mayest save me that am in bondage." Bondage can be easily understood to be exile in a Vermont attic, but it was wind—perhaps Amen's, or perhaps one of those late-summer cold fronts from across Lake Champlain—that blew a few of those funerary ashes away across the boneyard as George Mead covered the lost boy over, proving once again that life has plenty of moments of accidental poetry.

FALL IS ALSO THE SEASON FOR POLITICS AND country fairs, and it's hard to know which is which sometimes. As I write this, former governor Howard Dean is a candidate for U.S. president, and it's hard to put into words how scratchy and confused this has made most Vermonters. Dean served the state ably and without much in the way of pyrotechnics for eleven years, yet when we turned on the news at night we were stunned to see Our Boy pounding on the podium. "I represent the Democratic wing of the Democratic party!" he told the multitude, and Vermonters found this muddling, since we live in a state where political parties per se mean almost nothing. All sorts of people run for public office under all sorts of banners—the usual two, plus the Progressives, Liberty Union, Natural Law, Grassroots, Constitution, Socialist, and Reform. People who want to run and don't know what their party status is make up a new one pretty much on the spot—it's mostly a matter of printing up some letterhead—and if all else fails you can just be an Independent, like Congressman Bernie Sanders and Senator Jim Jeffords. Jeffords's switch from Republican to Independent in 2000 seems to have surprised everyone except his constituents, who are accustomed to this level of political spillage. According to the newspapers the Libertarians are even eyeing Vermont as the beachhead for their Free State Project, which is envisioned as an en masse political migration with an eye to some sort of takeover. Other rural states in their crosshairs include Wyoming, Idaho, and the Dakotas—as the Free State Project founder, Jason Sorens, once told a reporter, "I think it's time we concentrate our resources in a place where we have a shot at actually winning."

Sorens has a fun idea, but it won't work. What looks welcoming to him from a distance might prove disconcerting up close. It's an open system here, full of loose ends and static and crowded, happy fields of people who have no hope or even intention of winning, but do like being candidates and being on TV; throwing in a few more Libertarians will only add to a racket that was deafening to begin with. This carnival air exasperates some of the state's more serious politicians, but, like the Fred Tuttle candidacy, it is essentially a mechanism for unstuffing shirts. The Libertarians will fit right in, of course, but their notion of taking over a hick state with no electoral competition is just proof that not enough homework has been done. *Having a shot at winning* is not really what drives the process anyway; the sport lies in running.

This is why it wasn't Dean's candidacy itself that was unsettling, but the news that Dean thought he was an actual Democrat. When he was governor he looked like a fiscal conservative, which everybody liked; a generic social liberal, he didn't really support civil union for gays and lesbians so much as he accepted it, and he was willing to sign the legislation because it was a decent and fair thing to do. But what he mainly had—and I bet he still has—was an amazing collection of neckties, with blotches and dancers and zigzags and explosions of primary colors, and this made it interesting to watch the governor even if the viewer was bored by public policy. When you live in a state with a weak party system, you can vote your conscience and wear what you want. Like the smell that arrives by Labor Day, there's something essentially Vermont in this configuration.

Lots of people don't realize that Howard Dean is not the only Vermont candidate in recent history to try for the nation's top office. In the 2000 election Dennis Lane of East Warren ran for president on the Grassroots ticket but only after having picked up campaign experience in his runs for governor and secretary of state. His platform was primarily pro-marijuana, and he offered voters the unusual credential of having once sold a plasma lamp to the Grateful Dead. He explained to the *Valley Reporter* that he wanted to run "so I can vote for someone I trust with real solutions to problems," which, when you think about it, isn't really such a dumb idea, just stoned. But Lane has his finger on something that tumbles around happily inside the gestalt: At least half the time the phrase *party politics* refers to the difficulty of persuading the university students in Burlington to quit hollering and go to bed at a decent hour. They don't want a two-party system either; they want to party every night.

THE COUNTRY FAIR IS ANOTHER AUTUMN INSTITUTION with a big following. The essential elements—ox pulls, livestock judging, trotting races, country music, and a midway full of booths and rides—proceeds against a background of fried dough and overflowing litter cans and the occasional loose terrier. The grandstands are hard and the cotton candy blue and soft; strollers with protesting toddlers strapped inside bounce over the tussocky ground, and a great many helium balloons escape to freedom in the hard, flat blue of the September sky. Because I am afraid of heights, I avoid the Ferris wheel—just looking at a Ferris wheel makes me queasy—and stick to the FFA and 4-H barns, the Morgan horses, the quilts, and the food displays. Walking down the shed rows, you can do a meet-and-greet with a great many inquisitive descendants of Justin Morgan and admire their pointed ears and velvet noses. Of all of Vermont's offerings to the larger world, the Morgan horse may be the most durable and impressive, even if, in a typically Vermont manner, the founding of the breed was mostly accidental. It doesn't matter. The stubborn and practical beauty of a traditional, Vermont-bred Morgan trumps its origins on a schoolmaster's Randolph Center farm. Over the three days of the fair, the Morgans will jump, show extra gaits, pull carts, race around barrels, and win the walk-trot equitation class with a plump and incompetent first-grader on board.

The food displays look pretty boring at first—how many pies can you look at before they become interchangeable?—but there are strange layers of meaning going on in there.

Jan Albers offers, in *Hands on the Land*, the account of a farm wife in East Corinth who wrote, "I had an aunt that her husband didn't think he'd had breakfast unless he had hot apple pie. She was sick once and he came in the barn one morning and the hired girl was bustling around trying to have a pie ready for breakfast. And he told her she didn't have to bother . . . that they could get along without it. And my aunt, she was in bed, but she heard him say so. So, she said to herself, 'Old man, if the hired girl doesn't have to make pie, your wife doesn't have to.' So he didn't get any more pie for breakfast. He'd get it for dinner and supper but not breakfast."

It's that last sentence that reveals everything worth knowing about pie. Once you finish making one, it seems, you have to just go ahead and start making another. There was a time in northern New England when the Great Chain of Being depended on there being enough pies; the cooking displays, with their ribbons and honorable mentions, have surprising resonance in this context. But even the cooking, as always, takes a funny turn. A couple of years back, Linda Hemond, Wendy Huff, and Ellen Stark, all of Williston, took first, second, and third place in the Champlain Valley Fair Spam recipe contest with Spam stuffed shells, Spam summer noodle toss, and Spam curry puffs, respectively. Huff, when queried about her second-place finish, quickly conceded that winning the Spam contest might be seen by some as a peculiar victory, but then also observed, "If you can cook well with Spam, you can cook well with anything." The winner, Hemond, was proudly taking the top prize for the second time. A couple of years earlier, she vanquished all comers with a Spam angel food cake topped with maple frosting, a thing horrible to contemplate but obviously bakable.

If things like this are the regional cuisine, then so be it—it may be an actual improvement over that recurring mush that goes by the name of a New England boiled dinner. But an angel food cake with tinned meat in it does have a certain essential Vermont quality, an experimental willingness to fiddle around with pretty much anything, especially at the end of summer. When you can smell winter coming, even if it's still a few hundred miles away, then it's time to get your last or second-to-last licks in. Every fall the town of Peru, population 312, can apparently dip confidently into its resident pool and assemble a kazoo band on short notice for the annual Peru Fair parade, proving that the Peru Fair, though smaller than a bona fide county fair, still offers the bystander the requisite jolt of pleasure. "Those interested should gather at the town's west end parking lot at 9:00 A.M. to practice," says the call for volunteers. "Kazoos will be provided and suggestions for marching songs will be taken. Costumes, hats, and flamboyant scarves are encouraged." All this buzzing and flapping unfolds in late September, and one year it featured, among other things, a gorilla driving a tractor. The parade is described affectionately as a "town-long parade that turns around and comes back when it reaches the end."

THIS SWEET-AND-SOUR SEASON finally winds down when hunting season opens, and folks go off to camp with their flash-orange hats and their big boots and their clattering boxes of ammunition. It used to be that only the men went, but it seems that every year more women head off, too, and as far as I can tell they are entirely welcome and don't, necessarily, have to make a lot of pies. Mary Dunbar of Greensboro, who won't reveal her age but is known around Greensboro to be a great-grandmother, took a five-point, 122-pound buck a couple of seasons ago. It was mentioned in the paper mostly because it reestablished Dunbar as one of the area's most successful deer-slayers—she didn't get her buck last year, said the *Hardwick Gazette*, but she did for the five seasons before that. She told the reporter that her favorite gun is a .32 Special Glen she bought more than half a century ago for $27.

Killing Bambi's next of kin is an activity almost everyone in the state agrees on and approves of. If a conservative is a liberal who has been mugged, then a hunting advocate is an animal lover whose property has been nibbled raw by marauding deer. It's fun to hang around the game station where the deer are weighed, recorded, and checked for signs of illness. People come in from the woods smelling of tree resin and wood smoke and an indefinable cologne of adventure, and they handle the field-dressed corpses with remarkable reverence. They have stories, which they have to tell, about how and where they bagged this particular animal, and they look at their trophies with a slightly stunned admiration—these dead deer are exactly what they intended, but there is no feeling of triumph or smugness, only gratitude. One year I watched a bear come in. It was draped across the roof of a Subaru wagon with a fair bit of bear hanging over the edges, and there was something totemic about its black fur and its terrible stillness, as if some ur-bear, some god of all bears, had for some reason consented to come to town. It drew a nice crowd, excited but still respectful, and after a period of exclaiming over its size, everyone settled into a comfortable, trademark quietude. It was a fine, autumnal moment, one I'll always remember. We had gathered, it seemed, to offer the regal and innocent bear a decent farewell.

IT SEEMS ONLY FAIR:

A NOTE ON THE INDEX

IT SEEMS ONLY FAIR TO WARN YOU about this very weird index. The book contract was insistent: I was expected to produce an index, so I began building one after the first three or four chapters were written. Indexing is an honorable activity and surprised me by also being quite a lot of fun, but it became clear as I worked on it that the index for this book wasn't normal. For example, early on I found myself with what I believed was a completely responsible entry that said "Snowmen, exploding." This made me pause. In all my journeys through other people's indexes, I'd never seen anything that looked like that, but then I told myself, *Well, that entry will be hidden in a great heap of other, grown-up-sounding ones, and maybe no one will notice. It's unusual, but it needs to be in there and it's basically fine.*

The *Chicago Manual of Style* says that "a good index records every pertinent statement made within the body of the text." Later, it also says that the author "most nearly approaches the ideal as indexer," since the author "knows better than anyone else both the scope and the limitations of the work." This cheered me up—I liked being ideal, and I knew what was pertinent and the *Chicago Manual of Style* is always right. But then, at the end of a long afternoon of writing, I found myself putting in another index entry that read, "Bristol; beavers loose in; buried treasure in; dog behavior, mysterious in; shoplifting in; outdoor parties in; quarrels over laundry in." I looked at this entry for a long time with an indescribable mixture of delight and dismay, and also with a vague feeling that I'd actually seen something along these lines once before. Just before falling asleep that night I remembered—it had something in common with the index entries in Vladimir Nabokov's *Pale Fire*, a strange novel that is wrapped around a poem, an attendant and long-winded commentary, and all sorts of tantalizing front and back matter. The story floats, like a conjurer's silver dollar, somewhere between the rhyming couplets, the notes, the author, the reader, and, yes, a sly and merry index. I loved *Pale Fire*, but this was not a good situation.

Writers like to complain, so I e-mailed my editor, the intrepid Mary Norris. I told her what I just told you, but with a little more in the way of tears and hand-wringing; no situation is so bad that a writer can't find a way to make it sound more dismal. This worked, by the way. Mary e-mailed back immediately, saying, "I apologize for not discussing the index with you before now, as I don't think it's something we need for this book after all. Yes, it would be interesting to see if your home town was mentioned, but this is more a reading book than a travel guide, and presented as such it does indeed get a bit silly as to what episode should be indexed and what not."

Of course, the best and perhaps the only way to get a complaining writer to reverse her position is to agree with it; suddenly, perversely, I loved my index and wanted to finish it, and I wanted to see it printed. The problem now was how. Since I'd petitioned, obliquely, not to do it, and had been granted my reprieve, I wasn't sure how to reinstate the index without seeming ungrateful. How was I going to manage this? You would think that, working on a rather tight dead-line, I would have other things to worry about, but soon this became the *only* thing I worried about. The text of the book, I knew, was perfectly capable of taking care of itself, but the index, which suddenly seemed to me to be infinitely useful and really very charming, was in dire peril.

Of course, editors are usually in the right, and the *Chicago Manual of Style* also does say, the perfection of authors notwithstanding, that "authors are sometimes so subjective about their own work that they are tempted to include in the index even references to milieu-establishing, peripheral statements and, as a result, prepare a concordance rather than an efficient index." I didn't think I'd done that—I'd tried hard to make a pertinent index for an impertinent book—but just to be sure I showed a draft of my index to my sister and my brother-in-law when they came up to do a little skiing. "Does this look strange?" I asked.

"Do you really have a part in here about monsters?" asked Eric.

"I do," I said. "There's a whole long thing about that. There's a hairy monster in Northfield that goes through people's garbage."

"That sounds like a raccoon to me," he said.

"Maybe it is a raccoon—that's sort of what the chapter's all about. It's about needing monsters in our lives to assert our own civility." I paused. "I think."

I told them both about the park (see "The Edge of the Clearing") and showed them some blurry pictures I took of it the last time I was there. My sister Caroline, an artist and book designer, responded immediately to its otherworldly beauty. "Can we go there?"

This exchange lifted my heart—*can we go there?* is the final question I want the reader to ask, preferably on several levels—and it reinforced my conviction that the index had somehow assembled itself into being a legitimate signpost that belonged with the rest of the book. Granted, it points wildly in all directions, but a lot of the time so do I. If the goal of an index is to capture the intent of the author, then the very distractibility of it proclaims its legitimacy.

There are a lot of names in the index, but only one or two of them are famous, except maybe locally. For example, back last winter, I learned that Byron Kelly, the man who would have us count his apples, is actually the chief of police in Woodstock. Or maybe Byron Kelly is the chief of police's father; I was curiously timid about making the phone call to find out. Either way, I'm going to drive very politely in Woodstock from now on. Joe Citro is a widely respected Vermont author who collects stories of the paranormal, and Russell Banks and Pat Leahy are both pretty big deals. But if this book is about anything, it is about the courage, inventiveness, and personal momentum of people you've never heard of. David Frary and Bill Schubart and Terry Prue all matter and deserve to be alphabetized right along with the important folks. They ought to be able to tell their friends—modestly, of course, perhaps in the paper-towel aisle of the grocery store—that they have been included in an index. And if any of them ever writes anything that needs an index, I hope they will return the favor and include me.

INDEX

ABOUT THE AUTHOR

HELEN HUSHER IS A FORMER COLUMNIST FOR *Seven Days*, and her articles and stories have appeared in *Vermont Life*, *Vermont Magazine*, and other regional publications. She is also the author of *Off the Leash: Subversive Journeys Around Vermont*, which Kirkus Reviews described as "entertaining, well written . . . [and] likely to inspire more than one vacationer to retrace her steps." She lives in Montpelier, Vermont.